SYRIA

Recipes by **EMILY LYCOPOLUS**
Photos by **DL ACKEN**

SYRIA

RECIPES
FOR OLIVE OIL AND
VINEGAR LOVERS

TOUCHWOOD EDITIONS

CONTENTS

INTRODUCTION

Situated in a region rich in history and tradition, Syria is bursting with culture and diversity. Positioned on the Mediterranean Sea, and bordered by Turkey to the north, Iraq to the east, and Jordan, Israel, and Lebanon to the southwest, it embodies the notion of diversity, with its abundance of cultures, traditions, and religions—Islamic, Christian, Jewish, and Syrian Kurd to name but four. It also encompasses two of the world's most ancient cities, Aleppo and Damascus, but perhaps most notably, it is called home by a group of people who have a shared history of facing and surmounting adversity, and who celebrate life through an appreciation of food.

The importance of Syria's role in the development of global trade is reflected in the fact that it was the first country to have a foreign consulate on its soil—way back in the 17th century. However, it is worth noting a few significant points about Aleppo's contribution.

Aleppo marks the terminus of the ancient trading network the Silk Road, and it is the site of the world's largest covered market, the Al-Madina Souq, which is a full eight miles (13 kilometers) long. For decades it was world-famous for its dizzying array of goods—spices, silk, perfumes, tools, leather wares, ceramics, and jewelry. Goods would arrive in Aleppo from China and India before being traded and sent to Europe. It also formed the world's first trade agreement with the city of Venice in the 13th century and retained its position as one of the world's most important commercial cities until the Suez Canal was officially opened in 1869. As other forms of transporting goods developed, Aleppo's status as a major trading hub gradually faded.

However, Syria's influence over us remains, even if we're not aware of it. Many dishes that are commonly associated with Mediterranean countries, for example, actually originate from Syria. Greek dolmades and baklava, Italian panna cotta, Scotch eggs, cabbage rolls, and even mortadella are just a few of the many dishes with Syrian roots. Something I found fascinating during my research into Syrian food and culture is that because of the number of different cultures and religions in the country, there are also several "days of rest." This means that food vendors learn to cook the foods of their compatriots from different cultural backgrounds so that everyone can eat well, even on days when they are forbidden from working (which includes cooking). If you ask me, this takes living in harmony to a whole new level.

And I have to say, Syrians love their national cuisine. In fact, they are so proud of it that books of love poems have been written about it! One notable feature is that it is definitely a culinary tradition with an emphasis on sharing. I experienced this first-hand when I was living in Germany and attending language classes. My deskmate, Marawa, was a professor of psychology at the University of Damascus. Her family had arranged for her to marry a Syrian living in Germany so she could escape the country due to the unrest. Even though we couldn't speak each other's languages, we became fast friends. We hosted class parties in our homes, shared cooking ideas, and laughed our way through the language barrier in the most delicious fashion. It was the perfect way for us to practice our German, for her to practice English, and for me to learn some Arabic. Through that class, and especially through Marawa, I met many lovely Syrian people, each of whom was very welcoming and eager to feed me and my husband, Steve. Every time we dined with our Syrian friends an endless stream of dishes would emerge from the kitchen.

I remember one day when a new friend, Merih, invited us over for lunch. After a delicious meal of flatbread, hummus, salads, kibbeh, rice, roasted lamb, and much more, we looked at all the family pictures. Then we tucked into another round of fruit and sweets and enjoyed more lively conversation. Then Merih went into the kitchen and started preparing another round of dishes. We were still learning Syrian customs, and we mistakenly assumed that we could have lunch with Merih at noon and meet with *another* friend for dinner. We had no idea how on earth we could break the news to Merih that we had to leave, but we didn't know how to cancel our dinner plans either—as it was well after six in the evening, never mind the fact that we were so stuffed there was no way we would have been able to also eat dinner!

Years later, when we decided to start teaching cooking classes at our olive oil store, one of our employees mentioned that his dad was Syrian and really wanted to teach a class on Syrian food. I jumped at the chance. That class has been so loved by so many people here in our hometown of Victoria, BC, that we offer it twice as often as any other class. (Oh, and you might notice that I call for Greek-style thick yogurt in some recipes. It's a slight deviation from strictly traditional ingredients, but it was a purely practical decision in terms of accessibility.)

Syrian food is an accessible, diverse cuisine that I'm sure you will love discovering. To all of the warm and delightful Syrians who now call Canada home—we couldn't be happier that you're here and sharing your traditions with us.

LIME FUSED OLIVE OIL

Limes are one of my favorite citrus fruits. When faced with the decision of whether to add a dash of lemon, orange, or lime, I'm always going to choose lime. Created using the *agrumato* method—meaning the fruit is crushed alongside the olives while the oil is being made—this lovely Lime fused olive oil is bright, but subtle. The flavor of the lime zest comes through, as do the tart citrus juice flavors, and the brightness offsets the phenols in the olive oil, creating a taste that is quite simply unique. This oil is perfect in Syrian cuisine because although a pop of citrus is often used to brighten a dish, lime juice alone can be overpowering. This oil brings the flavor you need in a refreshingly delicate way.

HARISSA
INFUSED
OLIVE OIL

Harissa is actually a hot pepper paste. Here, the traditional harissa ingredients (red chili peppers, garlic, cumin, coriander, and caraway seeds) are infused into extra virgin olive oil, recreating the taste of the original paste but in oil form. This oil is perfect for frying and sautéing vegetables because the flavor permeates the entire dish (unlike the paste).

One small note of caution: the heat can really build with the Harissa infused olive oil. If you decide to make a meal that includes several recipes that call for this olive oil, I would encourage you to substitute the Lime fused olive oil in one or some of them. Especially if you are cooking for guests who are sensitive to heat and spiciness. At the very least, warn your guests and have an extra bowl of garlic yogurt sauce on hand.

POMEGRANATE DARK BALSAMIC VINEGAR

Thick, rich, bright, and tangy, Pomegranate dark balsamic vinegar is utterly delicious. The combination of pomegranates and balsamic vinegar creates something close to pomegranate molasses without needing to seed, crush, and boil 40 pomegranates, or use the often-over-sweetened versions found in our North American stores. This balsamic is incredibly balanced in terms of sweetness (from the grape must) and acidity (from the pomegranate).

The natural sugars in the balsamic make it ideal for caramelizing meat and vegetables. It works especially well in Syrian food—it's divine with salads—augmenting the traditional flavors of the region.

Sweet, tart, and fresh, Mango white balsamic vinegar is ideal for anyone who loves a pop of sweet brightness to make their everyday dishes a little more special. Created by crushing fresh mangos into white balsamic vinegar and straining out the pulp, this vinegar is as versatile as they come. Add it to sparkling water to make a refreshing drink, drizzle it over fresh greens for a quick and tasty dressing, or whisk it into yogurt for an easy fruit dip. Mango is commonly used in Syrian sweets and desserts, although I've loved incorporating this balsamic into some savory dishes as well to brighten up sauces and vegetables. It pairs perfectly with Harissa infused olive oil for a simple spicy salad dressing or marinade, and it meshes seamlessly with Lime fused olive oil to add a tropical note to a dish that needs some sunshine.

MANGO WHITE BALSAMIC VINEGAR

ESSENTIALS

ALEPPO SPICE
BAHARAT

In most Syrian cooking, a seven-spice blend of spices that many of us in North America would consider sweet is used to flavor both sweet and savory dishes. The foundation spice, allspice, is incredibly flexible and is delicious in everything from rice or milk puddings to ground meat and roasted vegetable dishes. Every household in Syria has its own version of this spice blend, so feel free to play with the ingredients to find the combination that is perfect for you. Some recipes call for galangal instead of ginger to make it even more fragrant, others add coriander and omit the cloves. In some parts of the Middle East, it's common to add paprika, and in Turkey, dried mint is used. The fresher the spices, the more flavorful the mixture will be—and if you use whole spices, toasting and grinding them yourself, the aromas will be intoxicating! Even though this blend is made from all dry ingredients, it pairs perfectly with the complexity of the olive oil and vinegars used in this book and is an essential ingredient in many of the recipes. In fact, I've included it as a standalone recipe because I use it so often.

Makes ½ cup

1½ Tbsp ground allspice

1 Tbsp ground cinnamon

1 tsp ground black pepper

1 tsp ground cardamom

1 tsp ground nutmeg

½ tsp ground cloves

½ tsp ground ginger

———————————

Place all the spices in an airtight jar. Shake to mix well. You can store this in an airtight container at room temperature for up to 6 months.

SYRIAN RED PEPPER PASTE

Just like Aleppo Spice (page 13), this red pepper paste is an essential pantry item in Syrian kitchens. The sweetness of the roasted red peppers mixed with the tangy sweetness of the pomegranate balsamic make this red pepper paste lovely whipped into yogurt for a simple dip, or used on its own as a sandwich spread. I always have a batch of this in the fridge and I'll often quadruple the recipe when red peppers are in season in the summer, so that I always have lots on hand.

Makes 2 cups

8-10 roasted red bell peppers

2 Tbsp Harissa infused olive oil

1 (5½ oz) can tomato paste

¼ cup Pomegranate dark balsamic vinegar

1 tsp sea salt

Slice the peppers into strips. Place the olive oil in a small saucepan and add the peppers. Sauté for 5–7 minutes, until just starting to break down and sear on the outside.

Add the tomato paste, balsamic, and salt, and cook for 3–4 more minutes, until the sauce is thick and chunky.

Scrape the sauce into a blender or food processor, and blend to form a thick and creamy paste. While it doesn't need to be completely lump-free, do try to get it as smooth as you possibly can. Alternatively, use an immersion blender to blend the sauce right in the saucepan.

Transfer to an airtight container and allow to cool completely. You can store this in an airtight container in the fridge for up to 3 months.

STRAINED YOGURT CHEESE
LABNEH

This Arab version of mascarpone, ricotta, and Greek-style yogurt is salty, and it's next to impossible to find here in North America. Luckily it's easy to make. Unlike homemade ricotta, it doesn't require cooking, just a long draining period. The Lime-fused olive oil lends a creaminess to the cheese, and a bit of tang to give this a little extra personality.

To make the labneh, in a large bowl, stir the yogurt and the salt together, ensuring that the salt is incorporated evenly through the yogurt.

Fold the cheesecloth into a 16-inch square at least two layers thick.

Spoon the yogurt into the center of the cheesecloth and pull the corners together. Tie the opposite corners together, not too tightly, so the yogurt can breathe, but tight enough that it will stay closed. Place the cheesecloth in a strainer with large holes over a large bowl and place a weight on top to help it drain. (My favorite way to drain it is to loop the knots over the tap in the kitchen sink, so the whey can easily drain. Pros: you don't need to place a weight on top. Cons: your sink is out of action for quite some time.). Let sit and drain for at least 12 hours, and no longer than 24 hours.

To store the labneh, spoon the mixture—it will be thick—into a clean jar with an airtight lid. Smooth the top and drizzle the olive oil over to seal. The Harissa infused olive oil can be quite spicy, so if you want to store this for a longer period, I would advise using the Lime fused olive oil here.

When you're ready to serve the labneh, spoon it into a serving dish, plate, or shallow bowl, and drizzle with your choice of additional olive oil, top with mint leaves,

Makes 2 cups

Labneh

2½ cups full-fat, Greek-style thick yogurt

1 tsp fine sea salt

1 large piece of cheesecloth

2 Tbsp Lime fused olive oil

For Serving

2 Tbsp Harissa infused olive oil or Lime fused olive oil

1 Tbsp freshly torn mint leaves

2 radishes (preferably watermelon, if they're in season)

1 seedless cucumber, sliced

½ cup pitted black olives

and serve alongside thinly sliced radishes, cucumber, olives, and flatbread.

You can store this in an airtight container in the fridge for up to 10 days. Labneh is also often scooped into small balls and rolled in sumac, za'atar, pistachios, nigella (onion seeds), sesame seeds, or Aleppo pepper. These little balls are then perfect to add to a bowl of soup, spread on fresh toasted flatbread (page 25), or decorate a salad. To make labneh balls, scoop tablespoons of the cheese into your hands and gently form a ball. Roll each ball in your spice of choice, nuts, or seeds. These will keep in an airtight container for up to 1 week in the fridge, ready to enjoy at a moment's notice.

TAHINI GARLIC YOGURT SAUCE

This addictive sauce is always in my fridge. Ok, it's never actually in the fridge, because it goes on everything and we're always running out. In fact, our household of two is now purchasing the largest tubs of yogurt and tahini available at our grocery store. You'll find this sauce in lots of recipes in this book, so do take the time to try it.

The order of ingredients here is important, so don't be tempted to just dump and whisk everything together. The many, many times I've ignored my own advice and done just that, the result hasn't been quite as good as it is otherwise. The reason is that the tahini clumps together and doesn't blend well with the yogurt, creating a slightly grainy texture in the sauce. Mixing the hot water and tahini together first loosens and softens it, so it is perfectly ready to be incorporated into the yogurt, making the silkiest of sauces.

In a small mixing bowl whisk the tahini with the water to form a very loose paste. Now whisk in the olive oil, lime juice, cumin, and salt. Grate or crush the garlic over the bowl, and then whisk it in as well. Add the yogurt and stir in to fully incorporate it into the tahini mixture, making an extra-smooth (that means no lumps at all!) sauce.

You can store this in an airtight container in the fridge for up to 10 days, although I'd love to see it last that long!

Makes 2 cups

½ cup tahini

¼ cup boiling water

2 Tbsp Lime fused olive oil

2 Tbsp lime juice

1 tsp ground cumin

½ tsp sea salt

1 clove garlic

1 cup full-fat, Greek-style thick yogurt

PICKLED TURNIP

Pickles are a staple in Syria, and you'll find them served with almost every meal. The mixture of turnip and beet is a classic combination that's used on falafel sandwiches, served with mezze, and really anywhere that you want to provide an added crunch to any bite. You'll lose yourself in the unique mix of slightly sour, hot, and sweet—the Mango white balsamic vinegar adds a lovely subtle sweetness and a flavor guests can't quite put their finger on, yet also can't resist. And of course, the turnips turn a rosy pink color from the beets, making this look as fabulous as it tastes.

Makes 4 cups

2 large turnips

1 red beet

3 garlic cloves

1 cup white wine vinegar

2 Tbsp lime juice

2 Tbsp Mango white balsamic vinegar

1 Tbsp pickling salt

Peel the turnips and the beet and slice them all into small matchsticks. Slice the garlic as thinly as possible into matchsticks (a mandoline is perfect for this).

Place the turnips, beets, and garlic in a clean 4-cup mason jar, packing everything in tightly while keeping the turnips, beets, and garlic evenly distributed.

In a small saucepan, place the white wine vinegar, lime juice, balsamic, and salt. Bring this liquid to a rolling boil over medium-high heat, let it boil for a full minute, and then pour into the jar. Leaving ¼–½ inch of headspace, top the jar with boiling water to ensure that the turnips and beets are fully covered. Seal the jar with its lid and ring and allow to cool to room temperature on the counter. If the jar seals, it can stay at room temperature for up to 3 months; if it doesn't seal, store it in the fridge.

The pickles will be ready after sitting for 1 week. Always refrigerate after opening. These will keep in the fridge for 6–8 weeks after opening.

How can you tell if your jar has sealed? If the dimple on the lid of the jar is depressed, the jar is sealed and taut. If the jar is not sealed, you'll be able to press the dimple in the lid down and it will feel quite flexible. If the jar has not sealed within 12 hours, you can submerge it in a pot of boiling water to boil for 20 minutes. Remove from the hot water and allow to cool to room temperature. As the jar cools, it will seal.

FLATBREAD

This simple bread is the perfect vehicle for a falafel or kebab sandwich, or for sopping up the remnants of soup. Using the Lime fused olive oil gives you a light, citrusy loaf that is ideal for subtle, milder dishes. Using the Harissa infused olive oil gives you a rich spicy loaf that is perfect with beef stews, Stuffed Meatballs (page 45), Baba Ganoush (page 41), and Tahini Garlic Yogurt Sauce (page 21).

In the bowl of a stand mixer fitted with the dough hook, place the flour and salt.

In a separate bowl or large liquid measuring jug, place the sugar. Pour the warm water over top and stir until the sugar is dissolved. Sprinkle the yeast on top of the water mixture and let stand for 3–5 minutes, until the yeast is dissolved and has started to froth.

Pour the yeast mixture into the flour mixture, scraping out any extra yeast that may be stuck to the side of the bowl. Add the olive oil and turn the mixer onto its lowest setting for 8–10 minutes, watching the dough to ensure that it is fully incorporated. You may need to scrape down the sides of the bowl once or twice.

If the dough seems overly dry, add 1–2 tsp of water, although I've never had to do that.

Once the dough is smooth and elastic, remove the dough hook, drizzle a little bit of olive oil over the dough, and turn the dough to coat it evenly in the oil. (At this point you can freeze the dough for later, if you like.) Cover with a dry tea towel or plastic wrap and let rise in a warm, draft-free spot for 25–30 minutes, or until doubled in bulk.

Gently dust a cookie sheet with flour and set aside.

Divide the dough into 6–8 pieces (depending on how large you'd like the finished loaves to be) and form each piece into a ball. Place each ball on the floured cookie

SERVES
FOUR

---

4 cups all-purpose flour

1 tsp fine sea salt

2 Tbsp granulated sugar

1½ cups warm (165–180°F) water

2 tsp quick-rising yeast

⅓ cup Lime fused olive oil or Harissa infused olive oil + extra for brushing and greasing the bowl

I love to brush the dough with a touch of olive oil right before I put it in the oven and sprinkle with za'atar or sumac to add a little extra flavor, especially if I'm enjoying the loaves on their own.

sheet. Dust them gently with flour, cover with a dry tea towel, then let rise for another 25 minutes, until the balls have risen until doubled in bulk.

Preheat the oven to 450°F. Place an oven rack in the second-lowest position. If you have a pizza stone, place it in the oven to warm. If not, thoroughly grease a second cookie sheet and set aside.

Once the dough has risen, gently form one ball at a time into an 8–10-inch circle with your hands. They don't need to be perfectly round, they can be very rustic-looking, and if they have lots of dimples, that's a good thing. Place the flattened dough on a floured surface. If you're adding spices, brush the dough with a little bit of olive oil and sprinkle the spices over top.

Working with one ball of dough at a time, gently place the dough on the oiled cookie sheet or hot pizza stone and bake for 5 minutes. The dough will puff up and turn slightly golden around the edges, although it will still be quite pale in color. As long as it looks pillowed, it will be cooked through. Lift the loaves off the tray or stone with tongs and set on a cutting board to rest, stacking them on top of each other so they keep warm. If you didn't add any spices to the loaves, brush them with a little bit of olive oil as soon as they come out of the oven.

Serve immediately. (I like to wrap them in a tea towel to keep them warm on the table.)

You can store these in an airtight container for up to 3 days, although they're best enjoyed the day they are made. They are also delicious in fattoush salad (page 67) if they've gone a bit stale.

You can store the unrisen, unbaked dough in an airtight container in the freezer for up to 2 months. When you're ready to bake it, let it thaw and rise in the fridge, then shape and bake as above.

CLASSIC ALEPPIAN RICE PILAF

Rice is a highly valued grain in Middle Eastern cuisine simply because historically it was difficult to obtain. In Aleppo, the main trading center, many types of rice were available, hence the name of this dish.

The Lime fused olive oil adds a lovely but subtle and refreshing flavor to this dish, and the aroma is remarkable.

———————————

In a frying pan with a lid, warm the oil over medium heat and then add the rice. Toast the rice until it is fully translucent and has absorbed all the olive oil, 1–2 minutes. It's crucial to stir it constantly during this time.

Pour in the water, add the saffron, and stir a few times to fully incorporate. Increase the heat to high, and bring the water to a boil. As soon as it starts to boil, turn down the heat to its lowest setting, cover the pan, and let cook for 30–45 minutes, or until the rice has absorbed all the water and is fluffy on top.

Gently poke a few holes in the top of the rice, but don't press down to the very bottom, to release the steam. Cook for an additional 10–15 minutes, still on the lowest-possible setting, with the lid tipped a little to release any extra moisture from the pan. Using a wooden spoon, carefully check the bottom of the frying pan. The rice should be golden brown with a thick, toasted crust on the bottom. If it's not completely golden, continue to cook on low heat for up to 15 more minutes, watching it closely and checking every few minutes so it doesn't burn.

Remove from the heat, remove the lid, and place a serving plate over top the pan. Turn it upside down over the serving plate—the rice should release in one piece. If desired, fluff the rice, mixing in the crusty bottom for some crispy texture throughout.

SERVES
SIX

Makes 4-5 cups of cooked rice

¼ cup Lime fused olive oil

2 cups short-grain rice
(basmati or jasmine work well)

3 cups water

6-8 strands saffron

A fun twist on this classic dish that is often served on Syrian tables is to add vermicelli to the rice. To make the dish this way, add 1 cup of broken vermicelli noodles to the oil and toast before adding rice. Be careful when the noodles are toasting as they do burn easily, so keep an eye on it.

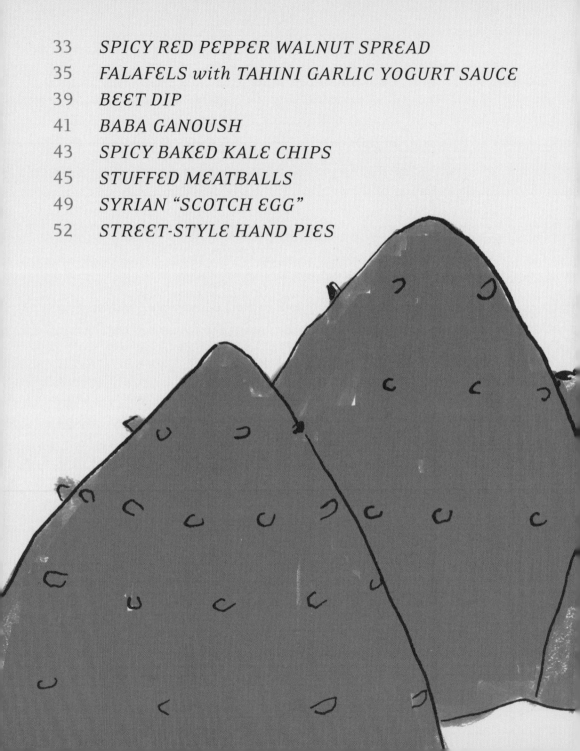

MEZZE

SPICY RED PEPPER WALNUT SPREAD
MUHAMMARA

Bright red and spicy all over, this dip is completely dependent on the quality of your Syrian Red Pepper Paste (page 15). If you like a little more heat, add a sprinkle more Allepo pepper. If you're keen to tone down the heat, omit the Aleppo pepper altogether and replace half the Harissa infused olive oil with extra virgin olive oil. But before you make that swap, know that the Harissa infused olive oil brings together the flavor profile and ensures a really even taste. The Pomegranate dark balsamic vinegar adds a sweet tangy component that is almost, but not quite, citrusy.

———————

Slice the roasted red peppers in half, and remove any residue seeds. Gently pat dry, then chop the peppers into small pieces. Roughly chop the garlic.

Place the walnuts in a food processor or blender, and pulse until finely chopped. Add the peppers, garlic, red pepper paste, and breadcrumbs and pulse again to start to combine them. Add the balsamic, Aleppo pepper, Aleppo spice, and salt and pepper to taste. Pulse to blend, then, with the machine running on slow speed, slowly pour in the olive oil. Blend until everything is combined but the dip still has some texture to it. (Don't try to aim for perfectly smooth. The nuts will make this impossible, and the texture looks pretty anyway.)

Place in a serving dish and use the back of a spoon to form some dips and ridges, so the olive oil can pool.

Garnish with a drizzle of olive oil, walnut halves, mint leaves, and pomegranate arils, if desired.

Serve with fresh flatbread (page 25).

You can store this in an airtight container in the fridge for up to 1 week.

Makes 2 cups

2 roasted red bell peppers (store-bought or home-roasted)

1 clove garlic

1 cup chopped walnuts

½ cup Syrian Red Pepper Paste (page 15)

¾ cup dried breadcrumbs

2 Tbsp Pomegranate dark balsamic vinegar

1 tsp Aleppo pepper

½ tsp Aleppo Spice (page 13)

Sea salt and cracked black pepper

½ cup Harissa infused olive oil, plus more for drizzling

Walnut halves, mint leaves, or pomegranate arils for garnish (optional)

If you roast the bell peppers at home, remember to peel them and discard the seeds before using them.

FALAFELS with TAHINI GARLIC YOGURT SAUCE

Variations on the falafel abound: some are baked, some are made with chickpeas, and some are made with fava beans. The unique thing about Syrian falafel is that they look like baby donuts. The small hole in the center ensures they cook evenly and prevents them from being doughy or soft.

—————

Preheat the oven to 325°F. Line a baking tray with parchment paper.

Place the chickpeas on the prepared baking tray. Sprinkle them with the salt, drizzle with olive oil, and shake the pan to roll them around to coat evenly. Bake for 15 minutes, until dried and just beginning to turn golden.

Remove from the oven and transfer to the bowl of a food processor or high-powered blender. Chop the onion and garlic and add them to the blender, along with the cilantro and parsley, baking powder, coriander, cumin, and Aleppo pepper. Blend to form a thick, smooth paste. Slowly add the flour, 1 Tbsp at a time, pulsing after each addition to thicken the paste. The dough should be wet enough to easily hold together in a ball, but not so sticky that it doesn't hold its shape and sticks to your fingers.

Transfer the falafel mix to a bowl and set in the fridge to firm up, about 20 minutes. (You don't need to cover it unless you're going to let it sit in the fridge for longer than 20 minutes.)

Scoop a heaping tablespoon of the falafel mix into your hands and form it into a ball. Using a skewer or chopstick, poke a small hole in the center to create a doughnut looking shape. Set the falafels on a lightly floured baking sheet.

In a heavy-bottomed frying pan or Dutch oven, add 1 inch of extra virgin olive oil, and heat it to 350°F over medium heat. Fry the falafels 4–5 at a time (being careful

SERVES
FOUR
—————
Makes 16–18 falafels

1 (19 oz) can chickpeas, drained and rinsed

1 tsp sea salt

2 Tbsp Harissa infused olive oil

1 small red onion

2 garlic cloves

½ cup torn cilantro leaves

½ cup torn flat-leaf parsley leaves

1 tsp baking powder

1 tsp ground coriander

1 tsp ground cumin

½ tsp Aleppo pepper or chili flakes

¼ cup all-purpose flour

Exrta virgin olive oil, for frying

Tahini Garlic Yogurt Sauce (page 21)

not to overcrowd the pan) for 1–2 minutes per side, until they're a deep nutty brown color. Remove from the oil with tongs or a slotted spoon, and drain on a paper towel–covered wire rack.

Serve immediately with the yogurt sauce, plenty of flatbread, and a variety of pickles.

Falafels are best the moment they are made, although you can store them in an airtight container in the fridge for up to 1 week. Reheat them in the oven at 350°F for a few minutes.

Often recipes call for dried chickpeas that are soaked overnight. I prefer to use canned chickpeas and roast them a little to dry them out, because it's much faster than soaking. That said, you're welcome to do the former if you have a plethora of dried chickpeas at home. Take 1 heaping cup of dried chickpeas and soak them in plenty of cold water and 2 tsp of baking soda for 8 hours or overnight. Drain, and toss with 2 Tbsp olive oil and 1 tsp salt (see method). Use as directed in recipe.

BEET DIP
MUTABAL SHAWANDAR

A lovely addition to a table of mezze, this dip is bright and cheerful with its beautiful pink color! I often boil the beets for this, as it's less time-consuming, but roasting definitely allows the rich sweetness of the beets to develop. Whichever method you try, I recommend doubling the recipe and storing some in the fridge. This is the perfect companion to fresh veggies as part of a lunch or as a snack.

———————————

Peel the beets and cut them into quarters.

To roast them, preheat the oven to 400°F, wrap the beets tightly in aluminum foil, and roast until tender (a knife should slip in easily), about 45 minutes. Remove from the oven and allow to cool completely in the fridge.

To boil them, bring a saucepan of water to a boil over medium-high heat, add the chopped beets, and boil until tender (a knife should slip in easily), 15–20 minutes. Drain the beets and allow to cool completely in the fridge.

Roughly chop the garlic and place it in the bowl of a food processor. Add the cooled beets, pickled beets, and pulse to break them up a bit, then add the tahini, yogurt, balsamic, lemon juice, and salt to taste. Blend until combined but not completely smooth. The dip should have a bit of texture.

Spread on a serving plate or in a bowl, garnish with sprigs of parsley, a sprinkle of nigella seeds, and a hearty drizzle of olive oil. Serve with vegetables and flatbread (page 25).

You can store this in an airtight container in the fridge for up to 1 week.

Makes 2 cups

2 large red beets

1 clove garlic

2 large pickled beets or ¾ cup chopped pickled beets

2 Tbsp tahini

2 Tbsp full-fat, Greek-style thick yogurt

1 Tbsp Pomegranate dark balsamic vinegar

2 tsp lemon juice

Sea salt

Nigella seeds, pomegranate arils, and extra virgin or Lime fused olive oil if desired

Nigella seeds are frequently used in Middle Eastern, eastern Mediterranean, and Indian cooking. They are tiny black seeds that have a slightly spicy warm onion flavor and are a beautiful addition to many dishes. They are typically found in Mediterranean specialty stores or spice shops.

BABA GANOUSH

This classic, delicious dip is a staple at almost every meal in Syria. It's the perfect sandwich spread, a hearty falafel dip, and—let's be honest—an amazing treat eaten straight off the spoon. The roasted eggplant makes a silky smooth base; the yogurt and tahini add a creamy richness that is complemented marvelously by the warmly spiced Harissa infused olive oil. Enjoy this with flatbread (page 25), Spicy Red Pepper Walnut Spread (page 33), and Beet Dip (page 39) for the perfect dip experience!

SERVES
FOUR

1 large eggplant

2 garlic cloves

½ cup full, fat, Greek-style thick yogurt

¼ cup tahini

2 Tbsp Harissa infused olive oil

2 Tbsp lemon juice

Sea salt

Za'atar and Harissa infused olive oil for garnish

Preheat the oven to 400°F.

Poke the eggplant all over with a sharp knife and place it directly on the bottom rack of the oven. Bake for 30–35 minutes, until soft and the flesh is pulling away from the skin. Remove from the oven and allow to cool just enough to handle.

While the eggplant is cooking, place the garlic, yogurt, tahini, olive oil, lemon juice, and salt to taste in a food processor or blender and pulse to combine.

Slice the eggplant in half and carefully remove the skin. Place the flesh in the blender and purée until completely smooth and lump-free.

Transfer to a serving bowl, cover, and allow to cool in the fridge for at least 20 minutes, or up to overnight, before serving.

Serve with a sprinkle of za'atar and a hearty drizzle of olive oil.

You can store this in an airtight container in the fridge for up to 3 days.

SPICY BAKED KALE CHIPS

At my house, these are requested more often than traditional potato chips and popcorn on movie night! Massaging the dressing into the kale leaves breaks down the fibers, making them soft and supple, and baking them in the oven gives you the most delicious and crispy spiced chip. The Harissa infused olive oil adds a gentle heat and the Mango white balsamic vinegar brightens the bitter earthy flavor of the greens, creating a lovely balanced taste.

SERVES
TWO

1 bunch curly green kale
(8–12 stems)

1 clove garlic

¼ cup Harissa infused olive oil

1 Tbsp Mango white
balsamic vinegar

1 tsp lime juice

1 tsp ground coriander

¾ tsp ground cumin

Preheat the oven to 375°F.

Wash and pat dry the kale. Destem the kale and tear the leaves into pieces, about 2 inches square.

Crush the garlic using a garlic press and place it in the bottom of a large bowl. Whisk in the olive oil, balsamic, and lime juice, and then the coriander and cumin to gently emulsify. Add the torn kale and gently massage it with the dressing. It will turn a lovely glossy bright green.

Place a baking rack over top a baking sheet and evenly spread the kale on the rack. Drizzle any remaining dressing from the bowl over the kale, allowing the curls to pick up the drips.

Bake for 7–10 minutes, until just crisp and the edges are turning golden, and the center of the chips are no longer raw. (Note that if you're using a convection oven, and you find the chips are still a little raw, you can sit them under the broiler for 1–2 minutes to crisp up.)

Transfer to a bowl and eat immediately.

These do not store well and should be eaten the day they are made. That said, I don't think you'll have any problem wiping the bowl clean.

STUFFED MEATBALLS
KIBBEH

Kibbeh is a staple dish in Syrian cuisine. This bulgur-based treat is prepared a variety of ways. It can be baked or fried, in patty- or in ball-form, stuffed with meat or vegetables. Some Syrian cookbooks dedicate entire chapters to this endlessly diverse dish. In this recipe, the pomegranate balsamic adds a richness to the filling and helps to caramelize the meat and keep it tender.

———————————

Rinse the bulgur under cold water, then place it in a small bowl, add enough cold water just to cover it, soak for 10 minutes, and then drain.

Place half the ground meat in the bowl of a food processor or blender with 1 Tbsp of cold water and pulse a few times to begin to break it up. Add the drained bulgur, red onion, 1 tsp of the Aleppo spice, and salt and pepper to taste. Pulse a few times to blend everything and then process until you have a very creamy fine paste. The bulgur should be completely ground and mixed with the meat.

Transfer to a bowl, cover, and place in the fridge for a few hours (or the freezer for about 25 minutes) to chill and firm up.

In a frying pan over medium heat, place the chopped walnuts and 1 Tbsp of the olive oil. Using a wooden spoon, mix them together until the walnuts are fully coated with oil. Continue to stir for 2–3 minutes, until the walnuts are evenly browned. Remove from the pan and set aside in a medium-sized bowl.

Without cleaning the frying pan, place the remaining ½ lb of meat, remaining 1 tsp Aleppo spice, and salt and pepper to taste in the pan and brown the meat over medium-high heat. As the meat begins to brown, break it up with your wooden spoon so the meat is very fine.

Kibbeh paste

1 cup bulgur

1 lb lean ground beef or lamb, divided

¼ cup diced red onion

2 tsp Aleppo Spice (page 13)

Sea salt and cracked black pepper

Kibbeh filling

¼ cup chopped walnuts

4 Tbsp Lime fused olive oil

2 Tbsp Pomegranate dark balsamic vinegar

These make a hearty addition to any soup, stew, or braised meat dish. While they're usually added raw and cooked with the other ingredients, you can also add them to a finished dish once they've been cooked.

When almost all the pink is gone, add the balsamic and continue to sauté until it has been absorbed. Add the walnuts, sauté for 1 minute, then remove from the heat and transfer to the bowl the walnuts were in (so we're not using extra dishes!!) and allow to cool enough to handle.

When you're ready to make the kibbeh, line a baking tray with parchment paper and remove the kibbeh paste from the fridge or freezer. Scoop a heaping tablespoon into your hands and form it into a ball. If the paste is too moist and difficult to handle, put it back in the fridge for 20 more minutes.

Using your index finger, gently press down in the center of the kibbeh ball to form a small divot and gently separate the sides, making a little well. Take about 1 tsp of the meat and walnut filling, place it in the well, then gently press the edges of the ball together, completely encasing the filling.

Place each meatball on the prepared baking tray. Place the balls in the fridge for 30 minutes to rest. At this point, you can also freeze them. (Freeze them on the baking tray and then transfer them to freezer-safe containers for up to 3 months.)

Preheat the oven to 400°F.

Drizzle the stuffed kibbeh with the remaining 3 Tbsp of olive oil and shake the tray to roll them around slightly so they're well coated in oil. Bake for 7 minutes, shake the tray to roll them around a bit again, and then bake for an additional 5 minutes to ensure the outside is cooked and the inside is warmed through. (If cooking from frozen, cook for 12 minutes and then 10 minutes.)

Remove from the oven and serve immediately. I love to serve them with tahini garlic yogurt sauce (page 21) and simple Syrian slaw (page 81).

You can store the cooked kibbeh in an airtight container in the fridge for up to 1 week. Alternatively, you can freeze the filling and kibbeh paste separately for up to 3 months, or store them separately in airtight containers in the fridge for up to 3 days.

Preparing kibbeh with cooked meat rather than raw meat ensures that you won't find a meatball with a raw center.

In Damascus, it is common to find these meatballs filled with ground meat and pomegranate molasses. In Aleppo, butter and mint is a common filling.

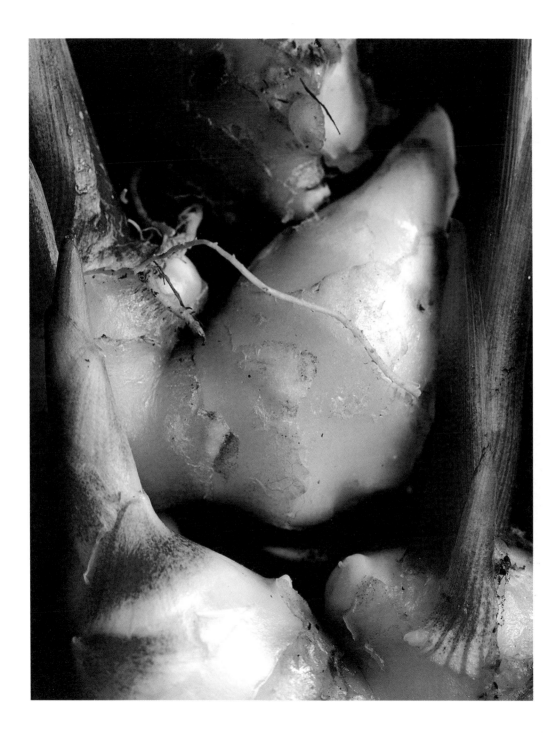

SYRIAN "SCOTCH EGG"
KIBBEH BAID

This isn't actually a Scotch egg, but one look at the photo will let you know why I've made the comparison. And guess what? This is one of those commonplace Western foods that originated in . . . Syria. (At the time of writing, a high-end department store in London was still claiming to have invented the Scotch egg, but there are many dissenting opinions about this.) Regardless of who invented this dish, know that originally it was designed to help use up leftovers.

Makes 6 eggs

8 eggs
1 recipe kibbeh
paste (page 45)
1 cup all-purpose flour
2 Tbsp Harissa infused olive oil
2 cups panko bread crumbs
Extra virgin olive oil for frying

Place 6 eggs in a saucepan of water and bring to a boil. Boil for 3–4 minutes if you like your eggs just set, 5–6 minutes if you like them well done. Rinse them in cold water and allow to cool completely in a bowl of cold water. Peel carefully and set aside.

Separate the kibbeh paste into six evenly sized pieces. Working with one piece at a time, roll each piece into a square on a lightly floured surface. Place an egg in the middle of the square and gather up the sides, encasing the egg fully in the kibbeh. Seal the kibbeh, doing your best to ensure there aren't any seams, set aside on a baking sheet (no need to line or grease it) and repeat with the remaining kibbeh and eggs.

Prepare a dredging station with three shallow bowls: one for the flour, one for the remaining 2 eggs, beaten with the 2 Tbsp olive oil, and one for the breadcrumbs.

Heat 2–3 inches of extra virgin olive oil in a heavy-bottomed saucepan to 325°F.

Roll one egg in the flour, coating it well and then dusting off any excess; dip it in the egg mixture, coating it well, and then dip it in the breadcrumbs, coating it well and then dusting off any excess. Repeat these steps with the remaining eggs.

When the oil is at temperature, fry the eggs in batches, 2–3 at a time, so you don't overcrowd the pan or allow the temperature of the oil to drop. Give the oil a minute or two to return to temperature between batches. Fry for 3–4 minutes, until golden brown, turning as needed to ensure they are evenly browned and cooked.

Remove from the oil and allow to sit on a paper towel-covered wire rack to drain. Serve warm or chilled.

These eggs are perfect with tahini garlic yogurt sauce (page 21), pickled turnip (page 23), dill pickles, and, to break with Syrian tradition, a lovely piece of English cheddar cheese.

You can store these in an airtight container in the fridge for up to 3 days.

STREET-STYLE HAND PIES

Hand pies are a perfect grab-and-go food. Pack this Syrian street-food favorite in lunches or in picnic baskets. The filling options are endless, but I've given you three of my favorites to get you started.

Lightly oil a mixing bowl with extra virgin olive oil.

Heat the milk until it is very warm to the touch.

In a large mixing bowl, whisk together 1½ cups of the flour, the sugar, yeast, and salt to fluff it all up and mix well.

Pour in the warm milk, add the egg yolks, and mix to form a soft dough. Scatter the remaining ½ cup of flour on the counter and turn the dough onto it. Knead for 8–10 minutes, until smooth and elastic. Place the dough in the oiled mixing bowl, cover with a dry tea towel, and allow to rise in a warm, draft-free spot for 15–20 minutes, until doubled in bulk.

Preheat the oven to 375°F. Line a baking sheet with parchment paper.

Divide the dough into eight balls and cover them with a damp tea towel. Roll the balls one at a time to a 5–6-inch disk about ¼–½ inch thick.

Place your filling of choice in the center. Carefully roll up the sides until they touch the filling and pinch the ends together, forming a boat shape. Place them on the prepared baking sheet.

Whisk the egg with a few tablespoons of water to form an egg wash and brush this over the surface of the dough.

Bake for 10–12 minutes, until golden and the filling is warmed through.

You can eat these warm or cold. If eating immediately, let them sit on a wire rack for a few minutes to cool before you dive in. You can store these in an airtight container in the fridge for up to 1 week.

Makes 8 hand pies

½ cup milk

2 cups all-purpose flour

1 Tbsp granulated sugar

1 tsp quick-rising yeast

½ tsp fine sea salt

2 egg yolks

1 egg

OLIVE AND ROASTED RED PEPPER HAND-PIE FILLING

BORAK ZAITOON

This filling is salty yet subtly sweet from the Pomegranate dark balsamic vinegar. It's packed with goodness.

———————

Finely chop the onion and garlic and sauté them in a frying pan with the olive oil over medium-high heat for 2–3 minutes, until soft and translucent. Pour in the balsamic and deglaze the pan, scraping up any bits from the bottom and allowing the onion to fully absorb the vinegar.

Slice the bell peppers in half, removing any extra seeds, then finely chop them and add to the onion mixture along with the olives, sumac, Aleppo pepper, and cumin. Sauté until the olives are just starting to brown and all the liquid has been absorbed. Remove from the heat and allow to cool. Use as directed in the recipe above.

You can store this filling in an airtight container in the fridge for up to 1 week. It doesn't freeze well.

Makes enough to fill 8 hand pies

1 red onion

2 garlic cloves

2 Tbsp Harissa infused olive oil

2 Tbsp Pomegranate dark balsamic vinegar

2 roasted red bell peppers

1 cup chopped pitted green olives

1 tsp sumac

½ tsp Aleppo pepper

½ tsp ground cumin

CHEESE HAND-PIE FILLING

Use this cheese filling to gives you hand pies that are classic comfort food. The Harissa infused olive oil kicks it up a notch by adding a lovely pop of flavor and color.

———————————————

Dice the onion and garlic. In a small frying pan over medium-high heat, heat 2 Tbsp of the olive oil and sauté until translucent and soft, 2–3 minutes. Remove from the heat and allow to cool just enough to handle in the pan.

In a bowl, whisk together the remaining 2 Tbsp of olive oil, the yogurt, and za'atar. Add in the onion-garlic mixture, scraping up any brown bits from the pan, and stir well to combine.

Slice the cherry tomatoes in half and add half of them to the yogurt along with the feta, mixing until the filling is combined and holds together. Use as directed in the recipe above.

Place the remaining tomato halves cut side up on the hand pies before placing them in the oven to bake.

You can store this filling in an airtight container in the fridge for up to 3 days. It doesn't freeze well.

Makes enough to fill 8 hand pies

1 red onion

2 garlic cloves

4 Tbsp Harissa infused olive oil

½ cup full-fat, Greek-style thick yogurt

2 Tbsp za'atar

½ cup cherry tomatoes

1½ cups crumbled feta cheese

BEEF FILLING
SFEEHAS OR FATAYER

This filling is hearty and utterly satisfying. The caramelizing effect of the balsamic sets it apart.

──────────────

Dice the onion and crush the garlic. Sauté them in the olive oil in a frying pan over medium-high heat for 2–3 minutes, until just translucent. Add the beef and brown it, breaking it up into fine crumbs. Add the Aleppo spice and Aleppo pepper, and then the balsamic and lemon juice and continue to sauté for 3–5 minutes, until the meat is completely cooked and all the liquid has been absorbed. Season to taste, remove from the heat and stir in the yogurt and tahini, then allow to cool completely. Use as directed in the recipe above.

You can store this filling in an airtight container in the fridge for up to 1 week. It doesn't freeze well.

Makes enough to fill 8 hand pies

1 red onion

2 garlic cloves

¼ cup extra virgin olive oil

½ lb extra-lean ground beef

2 Tbsp Aleppo Spice (page 13)

½ tsp Aleppo pepper

¼ cup Pomegranate dark balsamic vinegar

1 Tbsp lemon juice

½ cup full-fat, Greek-style thick yogurt

¼ cup tahini

Sea salt and cracked black pepper

SOUPS
&
SALADS

RED LENTIL and RICE SOUP

Hearty and warm, this soup is the best comfort food you could ever desire, especially on cold, damp days. Its thick texture comes from the rice, making it seem richer without the addition of cream or milk in the base. Served with a dollop of Tahini Garlic Yogurt Sauce (page 21) swirled in and a sprinkle of sumac on top, this soup is perfect for a crowd (the recipe doubles and triples easily) or enjoyed in bed with some flatbread when the first cold of the season strikes.

SERVES
FOUR

2 cups red lentils

½ cup short-grain rice

1 large yellow onion

2 garlic cloves

1 roasted red bell pepper

2 Tbsp Harissa infused olive oil

1 tsp sea salt

1 tsp ground cumin

½ tsp ground coriander

½ tsp ground allspice

½ tsp cracked black pepper

6 cups vegetable stock

Tahini Garlic Yogurt Sauce (page 21), sumac, and curly-leaf parsley (optional) for garnish

---

Rinse the lentils and rice together and then soak in cold water for 10 minutes. Drain and shake off any excess water.

Roughly chop the onion, garlic, and red pepper, and sauté in the olive oil in a frying pan over medium heat for 1–2 minutes, until just translucent. Sprinkle with the salt to allow the veggies to sweat and continue to cook and stir for 3–5 minutes, until the onions are very soft and just starting to brown. Add the lentils, rice, cumin, coriander, allspice, and pepper and toast for 2–3 minutes, until the rice is translucent. Add the stock, bring to a boil, uncovered, then cover the pan, turn down the heat to low, and allow the soup to simmer for 30 minutes, until the lentils and rice are fully cooked and very soft. Remove from the heat and allow to cool.

Working in batches, purée the soup in a blender, then return to the saucepan, and bring just to a boil, to ensure that the soup is hot enough to enjoy.

Ladle into serving bowls, and top with a dollop of garlic yogurt sauce and a sprinkle of sumac and freshly chopped parsley, if desired.

You can store this soup in an airtight container in the fridge for up to 1 week, or in the freezer for up to 3 months.

SPINACH and BEEF STEW with ALEPPO SPICE

I love making this in the slow cooker, as the spices intensely infuse the meat and fill your home with aromatic signs of delicious things to come!

Roughly chop the onions and thinly slice the garlic. In a medium-sized saucepan, heat the olive oil over medium-high heat and sauté the onions and garlic for 1–2 minutes, until just translucent. Sprinkle with the sea salt and continue to sauté for 2–3 more minutes, until just starting to brown.

Mix 1 Tbsp of the Aleppo spice with the beef and toss to coat. Working in batches, add the beef to the saucepan to brown on all sides. Deglaze the saucepan with 2 Tbsp of balsamic, scraping up any browned bits. Remove from the heat.

Place the beef in the bowl of a slow cooker and sprinkle the remaining 1 Tbsp Aleppo spice over top. Pour in the remaining ½ cup of balsamic and the beef stock, stirring to combine. Add the bay leaves, cinnamon stick, and cardamom pods. Cook on low for 5 hours.

At the five-hour point, wash and tear the spinach. Remove the whole spices from the slow cooker and add the spinach, gently stirring it to coat with the stock. Place the lid back on the slow cooker and cook for an additional hour to wilt the spinach and incorporate it into the stew.

Serve the stew in shallow bowls with flatbread (page 25) topped with za'atar or spoon it over classic Aleppian rice pilaf (page 29).

Garnish with lemon wedges, a sprinkle of sea salt, and pepper to taste.

You can store this in an airtight container in the fridge for up to 5 days. You can also freeze it—without the lemon wedges—in an airtight container for up to 3 months.

2 large red onions

4 garlic cloves

¼ cup extra virgin olive oil

1 tsp sea salt

2 Tbsp Aleppo Spice (page 13)

2½ lb stewing beef

½ cup plus 2 Tbsp Pomegranate dark balsamic vinegar

2 cups beef stock

2 bay leaves

1 cinnamon stick

4 cardamom pods

8 cups spinach leaves

Lemon wedges for garnish

Sea salt and cracked black pepper

To make this in the oven, prepare it in a Dutch oven or ovenproof pan and bake at 325°F for 2 hours, 20 minutes. Before serving, remove the spices, stir in the spinach, and let sit for about 5 minutes to let the flavors meld.

CHICKPEA SALAD

Full of protein and used in everything from dips and spreads to cold salads and hot dishes, the chickpea (which you may know as the garbanzo bean) is used all over the Middle East. This simple salad, which is best enjoyed on really hot days, showcases everything that is wonderful about this super-versatile legume.

SERVES
TWO

1 (16 oz) can chickpeas, drained and rinsed

1 red onion

2 Tbsp Lime fused olive oil

2 Tbsp lemon juice

¼ cup fresh chopped curly-leaf parsley

1 tsp sumac

Sea salt

Place the chickpeas in a serving bowl. Mince the onion and add it to the chickpeas. Drizzle the olive oil and lemon juice over top and toss to evenly coat. Add in the parsley and mix to combine. Top with sumac and sea salt to taste.

You can store this in an airtight container in the fridge for up to 1 week.

FATTOUSH SALAD

Most cultures have a version of a bread salad, and in this recipe, the crisp flatbread acts like a little chip, so you could make this salad into finger food if you like. I admit, there are a couple of non-traditional elements in this version, but together they make this is my favorite bread salad.

———————

Preheat the oven to 350°F.

Brush one side of each flatbread with 1 Tbsp of the olive oil per flatbread. Place on the bottom rack of the oven and bake for 5–7 minutes, until toasted and crispy. Remove from the oven and set aside.

In a large bowl, toss the arugula gently, tearing any large pieces, with the parsley and mint. Slice the cherry tomatoes in half, roughly chop the cucumber and fennel, slice the radishes and green onions, and add them all to the bowl.

Cut the flatbreads into 2-inch pieces, these can be shards or triangles, and sprinkle the pieces, as well as any crumbs, over the salad. Gently toss.

To make the dressing, grate or crush the garlic into a small bowl. Add the tahini, olive oil, lemon juice, balsamic, sumac, and salt and pepper to taste. Whisk to combine and drizzle over the salad ingredients. Using your hands, toss the salad, gently massaging the dressing through the leaves, ensuring everything is well coated.

Slice the avocado in half, carefully remove the pit, and roughly chop the flesh. Add it to the salad.

Divide the salad between two plates, top with cheese and sprinkle with za'atar.

Serve immediately. This salad is best enjoyed the day it's made, although the dressing will keep separately in an airtight container in the fridge for up to 1 week.

SERVES
FOUR
———

Salad
4 flatbreads (page 25)
2 Tbsp Harissa infused olive oil
4 cups baby arugula
1 cup chopped fresh
flat-leaf parsley
½ cup chopped fresh mint leaves
½ cup cherry tomatoes
1 English cucumber
1 bulb fennel
4 radishes (or 1 watermelon radish if they are in season)
4 green onions
1 avocado
½ cup fresh Strained Yogurt Cheese (page 17) or goat cheese
2 tsp za'atar

Dressing
1 clove garlic
¼ cup tahini
¼ cup Lime fused olive oil
2 Tbsp lemon juice
1 Tbsp Pomegranate dark balsamic vinegar
1 tsp sumac
Sea salt and cracked black pepper

TABBOULEH SALAD/PARSLEY SALAD

You might know tabbouleh as a bulgur salad, so prepare to learn something new. This classic salad is the very definition of an herb salad and it's commonly found on the lunch table. My dad would say it's rabbit food; I say, fetch the bunny ears! Feel free to play with the ratios and types of herbs, based on your personal preference or what is readily available in the garden. The Pomegranate dark balsamic vinegar adds a depth to the salad and complements the subtle flavor of the Lime fused olive oil. You can use curly- or flat-leaf parsley for this salad. Personally, I love the look of curly parsley, although flat-leaf is softer and more flavorful. The key is to avoid over-chopping the parsley and to ensure it's completely dry before you start to chop it. This prevents bruising of the herb, keeps the salad light, and prevents it from getting soggy too quickly.

———————————

Rinse the bulgur and place it in a small saucepan with 1 cup water. Bring to a boil, uncovered, over medium-high heat, allow to boil for a full minute, and then remove from the heat. Place a lid on top and let rest until the water is fully absorbed and the bulgur is tender, about 20 minutes. Fluff with a fork and let cool completely.

Wash and thoroughly dry the parsley and mint. Gently chop them and the green onions into small pieces and place them in a large serving bowl. Chop and rinse the tomato to remove the seeds. Add the tomato to the herbs and then mix in the bulgur.

Drizzle the salad with the olive oil, balsamic, lemon juice, Aleppo pepper, and salt and pepper to taste, then toss gently to fully combine without bruising the herbs.

Serve immediately. This salad is best enjoyed the day it's made.

SERVES
SIX

1 cup bulgur

1 cup water

4 cups chopped parsley

¼ cup chopped fresh mint leaves

3 green onions

2 Roma tomatoes

2 Tbsp Lime fused olive oil

2 Tbsp Pomegranate dark balsamic vinegar

1 Tbsp lemon juice

½ tsp Aleppo pepper
or ¼ tsp chili flakes

Sea salt and cracked black pepper

BULGUR SALAD
ITCH

In Aleppo, this salad is heavily spiced, filled with pomegranate molasses, and topped with pomegranate arils. Although delightful just eaten with a spoon, this is a great vegetarian option for filling lettuce cups.

SERVES

FOUR

2 cups bulgur
(white, if you can find it)

¼ cup Harissa infused olive oil

1 red onion

2 garlic cloves

1 tsp sea salt

1 cup vegetable stock

¼ cup (about half of a
5½ oz can) tomato paste

¼ cup Pomegranate dark
balsamic vinegar

1 tsp ground cumin

1 Tbsp Aleppo Spice (page 13)

2 Roma tomatoes

1 green bell pepper

1 red bell pepper

1 cup fresh chopped
curly-leaf parsley

½ cup chopped fresh mint leaves

Extra virgin olive oil,
za'atar, and ¼ cup pomegranate
arils for garnish

Rinse the bulgur in a fine strainer and then sit the strainer in a bowl of cold water to let the bulgur soak for 10–15 minutes. Lift the strainer out of the water, shake the bulgur dry, and set aside.

In a medium-sized saucepan over medium heat, place the olive oil. Dice the onion and garlic, add to the olive oil, and fry until just translucent, 2–3 minutes. Sprinkle with the salt and sauté until golden brown. Add the rinsed bulgur and, stirring constantly, toast for 1–2 minutes then add in the stock, tomato paste, balsamic, cumin, and Aleppo spice, stirring to combine. Bring to a boil. Allow to boil for a full minute and then remove from the heat, place a lid on the saucepan, and allow to sit for 30 minutes, until all of the liquid has been absorbed. Fluff the bulgur, transfer to a serving bowl, and allow to cool completely.

Dice the tomatoes, rinsing them to remove any seeds. Dice the bell peppers.

When ready to serve, add the tomatoes, peppers, parsley, and mint to the bulgur. Toss to combine. Garnish with a drizzle of olive oil, a sprinkle of za'atar, and pomegranate arils.

This salad is best eaten the day it's assembled. Leftovers can be stored for 1–2 days in an airtight container in the fridge, although the herbs will wilt and not be fluffy and fresh.

POTATO SALAD

Definitely a departure from the mayo-laden potato salads of North America, this is tart and crunchy and pairs perfectly with grilled meats, making it ideal for summer barbecues and potluck dinners. There are dozens of variations of this across the Middle East. In my version, the Harissa infused olive oil adds a healthy dose of heat to the salad, but if you're looking for something milder, use extra virgin olive oil—or try using Lime fused olive oil for a delicious twist.

———————

Bring a large saucepan of salted water to a boil over high heat. Cut the potatoes into bite-size pieces. Add to the water and boil until just fork-tender. Be sure you don't overcook them. Drain, rinse in cold water, and allow to cool slightly (but not completely—you need them to retain some heat).

In a large serving bowl, grate or crush the clove of garlic. Add the olive oils, lemon juice, Aleppo spice, salt, and pepper, and whisk to combine. Place the warm potatoes in the dressing and toss to coat evenly. Thinly slice the radishes, green onions, and dill pickles, add to the potatoes, and gently mix to combine. Top the salad with sliced hardboiled egg and sprigs of parsley right before serving.

You can eat this salad warm, or chill it, without the egg or parsley, for at least 4–6 hours to let the flavors develop fully.

You can store this—without the egg or parsley—in an airtight container in the fridge for up to 1 week.

SERVES
SIX

2 lb waxy potatoes, small or large (Yukon gold, red, purple, or fingerling)

1 clove garlic

2 Tbsp Harissa infused olive oil

2 Tbsp extra virgin olive oil

½ cup lemon juice

2 tsp Aleppo Spice (page 13)

1 tsp sea salt

½ tsp cracked black pepper

4 radishes

2 green onions

2 medium dill pickles

1 hardboiled egg

Sprigs of curly-leaf parsley for garnish

ROASTED CAULIFLOWER SALAD

Cauliflower is most commonly prepared in Syria as a mezze. However, this classic vegetable makes a roasted salad that is delicious, healthy, and heartwarming in the winter months. Drizzling it with Pomegranate dark balsamic vinegar and Tahini Garlic Yogurt Sauce (page 21) adds a creamy brightness to the dish that makes it utterly irresistible.

——————

Preheat the oven to 450°F. Line a baking tray with parchment paper.

Separate the head of cauliflower into small florets, place them in a medium-sized bowl, drizzle the olive oil over top, sprinkle with the cumin, and mix to ensure the florets are evenly coated. Arrange them evenly on the prepared baking tray.

Roast for 15 minutes, until the cauliflower is fork-tender and the tips are golden brown. Allow to cool completely on the baking tray.

When ready to serve, arrange the cauliflower on a serving plate. Drizzle first with the balsamic and then with the garlic yogurt sauce. Finish off with a sprinkle of sumac, parsley, and pomegranate seeds (in that order) to garnish.

Enjoy immediately. In theory you can store it in an airtight container for up to 3 days, although it will get soggy after a night in the fridge so it's best enjoyed the day it's made.

SERVES
TWO
——

1 large head cauliflower

¼ cup Lime fused olive oil

1 tsp ground cumin

2 Tbsp Pomegranate dark balsamic vinegar

½ cup Tahini Garlic Yogurt Sauce (page 21)

½ tsp sumac

2 Tbsp chopped fresh curly-leaf parsley

2 Tbsp pomegranate arils

OLIVE SALAD

It should come as no surprise that this salad is a mainstay in Syrian kitchens, as Syria ranks fourth in the world for olive production at time of writing and is arguably the home of the original olive tree. (See Julie Angus's book *Olive Odyssey* for more on this intriguing story!) Typically, olives are grown in the Harem region and in the Kurd Mountains, although they are found all over the country. For this salad, it's important to use the best quality olives you can find—not too salty, not soft and squishy, but very crunchy. I recommend you get to know your local deli counter assistant for help with this.

———————

Rinse the olives well in a strainer, shaking dry. Place them in a serving bowl.

Mince the onion. Dice the tomatoes, then rinse them to remove any seeds. Add the onions and tomatoes to the olives.

Whisk together the olive oil, red pepper paste, tomato paste, balsamic, and lemon zest to form a creamy smooth dressing. Season to taste with salt and pepper.

Pour the dressing over the olives and toss to coat well. Garnish with parsley and grated lemon zest.

This salad is a great one to have on hand as it will keep for up to 10 days in an airtight container in the fridge. It's perfect with strained yogurt cheese (page 17) for breakfast.

SERVES
TWO

10 oz pitted green olives

1 small red onion

2 Roma tomatoes

¼ cup extra virgin olive oil

2 Tbsp Syrian Red Pepper Paste (page 15)

1 Tbsp tomato paste

1 Tbsp Pomegranate dark balsamic vinegar

1 tsp lemon zest

Sea salt and black pepper

Parsley and grated lemon zest for garnish

———————

If you happen on a jar of olives that is too salty, rinse the olives well and then soak them in a bowl of cold water, uncovered, in the fridge for 12–24 hours to draw out the salt. Rinse and repeat, if necessary.

———————

CARROT SALAD

There is something so lovely about a bright crunchy carrot salad. This version has all the flavors of Levant and is often eaten in the early fall, when both the apples and root vegetables are ready, and the fresh greens in the garden are just beginning to wilt and go out of season. The Mango white balsamic vinegar adds a sweet freshness that is complemented by the honey and ginger, while the Lime fused olive oil creates a lovely subtle underlying citrus note that is heightened by the acid in the vinegar, the lemon juice, and, of course, the sumac. The mellow flavors of cumin and coriander even out the flavor and create the most delicious medley to top this cheerful salad.

———————————

Place the raisins in a small bowl and cover with boiling water. Let sit for at least 10 minutes to allow them to rehydrate and plump.

Grate the carrots into a large bowl, using a box grater with large holes. Peel and grate the apple and toss with the carrots. Crush the garlic and add it to the carrots with the ginger. Add the chopped cilantro leaves and toss again to combine.

In a small bowl whisk together the olive oil, balsamic, lemon juice, honey, cumin, coriander, sumac, and salt and pepper to taste. Pour this dressing over the salad and mix well to ensure that the salad is evenly coated. Drain the raisins, sprinkle them over the salad, and toss gently. Let sit in the fridge, covered, for at least 1 hour, or up to 12 hours, to allow the flavors to develop.

Right before serving, top with feta cheese and cilantro leaves to garnish.

You can store this in an airtight container for up to 3 days. (Any longer and the garnish will be too limp to enjoy.)

SERVES
FOUR
———

½ cup dark raisins

2½ cups grated carrot
(about 4 large carrots)

1 apple

1 garlic clove

1 tsp grated ginger

¼ cup chopped cilantro leaves

2 Tbsp Lime fused olive oil

2 Tbsp Mango white
balsamic vinegar

2 Tbsp lemon juice

2 Tbsp honey

1½ tsp ground cumin

1 tsp ground coriander

½ tsp sumac

Sea salt and cracked black pepper

½ cup crumbled Strained Yogurt
Cheese (page 17) or feta cheese

Cilantro leaves for garnish

———————

I like to use Granny Smith apples for this recipe but any type, with the exception of red delicious, works well. Red delicious go brown too quickly.

———————

SIMPLE SYRIAN SLAW

A simple cabbage slaw is never far from the table in a Syrian kitchen. Cabbage is hearty, easy to grow, full of nutrients, and easy to prepare in myriad ways. Use this slaw to make a falafel sandwich; spread it on a piece of flatbread (page 25) with Tahini Garlic Yogurt Sauce (page 21) and falafels (page 35) for a most delicious wrap; serve it on the side with Spiced Chicken Skewers (page 103); or use it as a refreshingly spicy mezza with a variety of other plates to go around. The Harissa infused olive oil definitely adds a kick to the slaw, so I've cut it with extra virgin olive oil. However, if you love spice, feel free to use Harissa infused olive oil instead of extra virgin. The Mango white balsamic vinegar tempers the spice with a welcome touch of sweetness.

SERVES
FOUR

1 small green cabbage

1 clove garlic

¼ cup Mango white balsamic vinegar

¼ cup lemon juice (about 2 large lemons)

2 Tbsp Harissa infused olive oil

2 Tbsp extra virgin olive oil

1 tsp ground cumin

Sea salt and cracked black pepper

Chop the cabbage into quarters and remove the core. Using a mandoline or sharp knife, slice the cabbage finely into thin strips.

Grate or crush the clove of garlic into a mixing bowl. Whisk in the balsamic, lemon juice, both olive oils, cumin, and salt and pepper to taste. Add the cabbage and mix well to ensure that the cabbage is well coated in dressing.

You can store this in an airtight container in the fridge for up to 1 week.

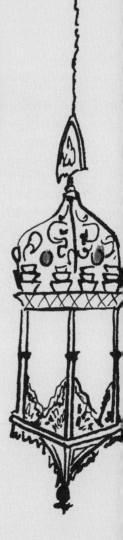

MAINS

FATTEH

Fatteh is a common breakfast food in Damascus, and there are many different ways to prepare it. The general idea is to top toasted flatbread with chickpeas, ground lamb, eggplant, or chicken. Drizzle it with garlic yogurt sauce, and a few extra pieces of crispy bread and toasted pine nuts.

———

Preheat the oven to 350°F.

Brush each piece of bread with 2 Tbsp of the Lime fused olive oil, using 1 Tbsp per side, and let it sit for a moment for the oil to be absorbed. Place the bread on a baking sheet and bake for 3–5 minutes, just until golden. Allow to cool enough to handle and then chop into roughly 2-inch-wide wedges. Line the bottom of two serving plates or bowls with half the pieces.

Slice the garlic finely. In a frying pan over medium-high heat, warm the remaining ¼ cup of Lime fused olive oil. Add the garlic and cook until it just begins to sizzle. Add the chickpeas, lime juice, Aleppo spice, cumin, salt, and pepper and cook until the chickpeas are soft and warmed through.

Divide the chickpeas between the two dishes to top the toasted bread.

Using the same frying pan (no need to wipe it out first), toast the pine nuts in the Harissa infused olive oil over medium heat, shaking the pan gently to keep the nuts moving. They burn quickly, so keep a close eye on them. When they are golden, remove from the heat and let rest in the pan for a few moments.

Drizzle the chickpeas with garlic yogurt sauce and top with the pine nuts, remaining pieces of pita, and the sumac. Garnish with parsley.

Serve immediately. The bread will get soggy, so this is best enjoyed as soon as it's assembled. Each individual component can be prepped ahead of time, though.

SERVES
TWO
———

3 pita or flatbread (page 25)

½ cup Lime fused olive oil, divided

2 garlic cloves

1 (19 oz) can chickpeas, drained and rinsed

2 Tbsp lime juice

2 tsp Aleppo Spice (page 13)

½ tsp ground cumin

½ tsp sea salt

¼ tsp cracked black pepper

½ cup pine nuts

1 Tbsp Harissa infused olive oil

½ cup Tahini Garlic Yogurt Sauce (page 21)

1 tsp sumac

Curly-leaf parsley for garnish

———

For a hearty dinner or Sunday brunch, add ½ lb of ground beef or lamb along with the chickpeas. Simple and delicious, this dish is a personal favorite— and it only takes a few moments to put together.

———

BRAISED BEANS with ALEPPO SPICES

These beans are the perfect side dish to almost any main. Try them with Spicy Baked Fish (page 97), Spiced Chicken Skewers (page 103), Lamb Shanks with Freekeh Pilaf (page 111), Eggplant with Minced Lamb and Pomegranate (page 109), or even Eggs Baked in Tomato Sauce (page 93). The trick to these lovely beans is to sauté them on high heat, so they blanch more than actually cook, and to whisk in the tomato paste and balsamic so the sauce clings like mud to the beans.

Trim the beans, wash well, and toss to dry in a colander. Crush the garlic cloves with the back of a knife, leaving them whole.

Place the olive oil in a frying pan over medium-high heat and sauté the beans and garlic cloves for 1–2 minutes, until the beans sear a little and the garlic softens slightly. Sprinkle with the Aleppo spice and salt, and pour in the stock. Bring to a boil and then turn down the heat and simmer, uncovered, for 3–4 minutes, turning the beans frequently, until the stock has reduced to 2–3 Tbsp and the beans are bright green.

In a small bowl, whisk together the tomato paste and balsamic. Pour this into the pan and continue turning the beans until they are fully coated in the tomato-balsamic sauce, 2–3 minutes. Remove from the heat and serve immediately.

You can store these in an airtight container in the fridge for up to 3 days, although they will lose their crispness, so they're best enjoyed the day they are made.

Serves two as a main, four as a side

2 lb green string beans

6 garlic cloves

2 Tbsp Lime fused olive oil

2 tsp Aleppo Spice (page 13)

½ tsp sea salt

¾ cup vegetable stock

1 (5½ oz) can tomato paste

2 Tbsp Pomegranate dark balsamic vinegar

STEWED FAVA BEANS
FOOL MEDAMMAS

Fava beans (or broad beans) are very versatile, and they are one of the oldest cultivated beans on the planet. Typically served for breakfast, these beans are traditionally prepared by cooking them in large clay pots or brass urns for 12 hours over an open fire. They are served in earthenware bowls as a street food. This is the perfect vegetarian dinner.

Place the fava beans, water, Lime fused olive oil, 1 tsp of the cumin, and the salt in a medium saucepan over medium-high heat. Bring to a rolling boil, stirring to ensure the beans don't stick. Let boil, stirring constantly, until only a few tablespoons of liquid remain, 4-6 minutes. Remove from the heat if the beans start to split. If a lot of liquid remains, remove the beans with a slotted spoon and test the beans to ensure they are warm. Allow to cool slightly, just enough to handle—you don't want them to be completely cold.

In a medium-sized bowl, whisk together the tahini and lemon juice, and then add the garlic yogurt sauce. Add the fava beans and stir to coat well.

Dice the tomatoes, rinsing them to remove any seeds. Dice the green onions.

Spoon the fava beans into two serving bowls, top with tomatoes, green onion, and parsley. Sprinkle with the remaining 1 tsp of cumin and the Aleppo pepper or chili flakes. Drizzle generously with the Harissa infused olive oil. Serve with a lemon wedge on the side for drizzling according to taste.

Serve with classic Aleppian rice pilaf (page 29) or flatbread (page 25) for scooping up the beans.

You can store these in an airtight container in the fridge for up to 5 days.

1 (16 oz) can fava or broad beans, drained and rinsed

½ cup water

¼ cup Lime fused olive oil

2 tsp ground cumin

½ tsp sea salt

2 Tbsp tahini

1 Tbsp lemon juice

¼ cup Tahini Garlic Yogurt Sauce (page 21)

2 Roma tomatoes

3 green onions

¼ cup chopped curly-leaf parsley

½ tsp Aleppo pepper or ¼ tsp chili flakes

¼ cup Harissa infused olive oil

Lemon wedges for garnish

If you want to keep this dish more on the mild side, feel free to use Lime fused or extra virgin olive oil for the final drizzle.

TOMATO POMEGRANATE-BRAISED STUFFED ZUCCHINI
MASHI

One of my favorite things about Syrian cuisine is that so many dishes are stuffed with various components. For me, this gives a lovely element of surprise to the dish—fun for guests and fun to prepare as well. Stuffed young zucchini is a traditional favorite. It can be braised in either a rich tomato sauce or a white butter sauce. Here I decided to use the tomato version, although both are so delicious. The Pomegranate dark balsamic vinegar balances the sweet acidity of the tomatoes and adds a brightness to the warmth of the spices.

SERVES
FOUR

½ cup long-grain rice

1 cup water

12 small zucchini

2 small yellow onions

½ lb ground beef or lamb

2 Tbsp + ¼ cup Pomegranate dark balsamic vinegar

2 Tbsp Aleppo Spice (page 13)

3 tsp sumac, divided

½ tsp sea salt

4 garlic cloves

2 Tbsp Harissa infused olive oil

1 (28 oz) can whole tomatoes

¾ cup beef stock

¼ cup freshly torn mint leaves

2 bay leaves

1 sprig of thyme

Sea salt and cracked black pepper

1 (5½ oz) can of tomato paste

Fresh mint leaves and a sprinkle of sumac for garnish

Place the rice in a small saucepan with 1 cup of boiling water over high heat. Turn down the heat to its lowest setting and simmer until the rice is fully cooked, about 20 minutes.

While the rice is cooking, slice the ends off the zucchini. Using a sharp paring knife or apple corer, carefully cut a small deep hole in the center of the zucchini to remove the seeds. Be careful not to break the flesh or cut right down to the other end. You're cutting an entrance for the stuffing, but no exit—so it doesn't fall out when being cooked.

Dice one of the onions, place it in a mixing bowl, and then add the beef, the 2 Tbsp of balsamic, the Aleppo spice, 1 tsp of the sumac, and the salt. Mix until fully incorporated. Fluff the rice, add to the pan, and mix well to form an even, thick stuffing. Carefully stuff each of the zucchini with the meat-rice stuffing. Don't push the stuffing in too hard as you want to keep the zucchini intact. Leave a ½-inch opening at the end.

Preheat the oven to 350°F.

Chop the remaining onion and the garlic.

In a heavy-bottomed frying pan or Dutch oven, sauté the onion and garlic in the olive oil over medium-high heat until translucent and soft, 3–4 minutes. Pour the juice from the can of tomatoes into the pan, then gently crush the tomatoes in your hand before adding them to the pan. Pour in the remaining ¼ cup of balsamic, the stock, the remaining 2 tsp sumac, mint, bay leaves, and thyme. Season with salt and pepper to taste.

Bring to a boil over medium-high heat and then whisk in the tomato paste. Allow to boil for 2 minutes then remove from the heat. Place the zucchini in an even layer in the sauce, with the cut ends facing the outside of the pan, and cover with a lid. Or arrange the zucchini in a roasting pan just large enough to hold them without crowding with the cut sides facing the edges and pour the sauce over top.

Cover and bake for 1 hour. Test the zucchini to ensure it is soft and the meat is fully cooked. The internal temperature of the zucchini should be 165°F. Remove the lid, and cook for an additional 15 minutes, so the sauce can reduce and the top can crisp.

Remove from the oven and let stand for 10 minutes before serving. Arrange the zucchini on a serving platter, drizzle with the sauce, and sprinkle with fresh mint and sumac.

You can store this in the fridge in an airtight container for up to 3 days, or in the freezer for up to 3 months.

Depending on the size of the zucchini, you might have some filling left over. You can brown this with the onion and garlic to make a meaty sauce for the zucchini to cook in, or make it into small meatballs to add to the sauce when you add the zucchini.

EGGS BAKED in TOMATO SAUCE
SHAKSHUKA

Eggs and tomato is a global dish, every country and culture have some rendition of these two ingredients together. This spicy Syrian rendition is warm, delicious, and beautiful to serve as a simple one-pot dinner, hearty brunch item, or easy side dish to add some protein to a veggie-heavy mezze table. Using the Harissa infused olive oil as the foundation fills this dish with a warm, present heat, while the Pomegranate dark balsamic vinegar adds a rich, sweet complexity to the sauce and balances the acidity of the tomatoes. Perfect harmony on a plate!

SERVES
FOUR

1 red onion

2 garlic cloves

¼ cup Harissa infused olive oil

1 tsp sea salt

½ lb ground beef

1 tsp Aleppo Spice (page 13)

2 tsp ground cumin

1 tsp cracked black pepper

2 red bell peppers

1 (28 oz) can whole tomatoes

¼ cup Pomegranate dark balsamic vinegar

¼ cup (half a 5½ oz can) tomato paste

4 eggs

½ cup Strained Yogurt Cheese (page 17) or feta cheese

Curly-leaf parsley for garnish and an extra drizzle of Harissa infused olive oil

Dice the onion and crush the garlic. In a cast iron frying pan or heavy-bottomed frying pan over medium heat, place the olive oil, add the onions and garlic, and sauté until just translucent. Add the salt and continue to sauté for another 2–3 minutes, to let the onions sweat and just start to turn golden. Add the ground beef and begin to break apart the meat to brown evenly. Increase the heat to medium-high. Add the Aleppo spice, cumin, and pepper and continue to sauté for 5–7 minutes, until the meat is fully browned.

Roughly chop the peppers and add them to the meat mixture, stirring to combine. As the peppers just begin to soften, about 5 minutes, open the can of tomatoes leaving a part of the lid intact. Holding the lid down gently, pour the tomato juice from the can into the pan. It will instantly sizzle and then, as it warms up, begin to bubble gently. Turn down the heat to medium, then, using a butter knife or fork, carefully lift the lid from the top of the can and dump the tomatoes into your hand, crushing each tomato gently to break it apart before adding it to the sauce. Mix in the tomatoes, breaking them apart even more as you stir. As the sauce begins to reduce, add the balsamic, bring to a boil, and then turn down the heat to simmer for about 5 minutes, allowing the sauce to start to thicken. Add the tomato paste, stirring the sauce constantly for the next 2–3 minutes, ensuring that the sauce is thick and fully incorporated.

If you want to make this dish in advance, this is the spot to stop. (Allow the sauce to cool and then pop it in the fridge until you're ready to serve it.)

When ready to serve, bring the sauce back up to a strong simmer over medium-high heat, ensuring it is fully warmed (especially if it's coming from the fridge). Turn down the heat to its lowest setting and make four 2–3-inch wells or divots in the sauce, but be careful that the bottom of the pan is not showing. Crack one egg into each well, cover the pan, and simmer for 4–5 minutes for soft yolks, 6–7 minutes for firm yolks. Remove from the heat and let rest 2–3 minutes, uncovered. Sprinkle with the strained yogurt cheese, and garnish with curly-leaf parsley and a drizzle of olive oil. Serve family-style with lots of flatbread for scooping up the extra sauce.

This dish doesn't keep well after the eggs have been added and it's been fully prepared. That said, the tomato sauce by itself stores wonderfully well. You can store it in an airtight container for up to 1 week in the fridge or for up to 3 months in the freezer.

To make this vegetarian, omit the ground beef and add an extra red bell pepper and a small zucchini or eggplant chopped into 1-inch cubes.

SPICY BAKED FISH

This simple crowd-pleaser is bursting with the warmth of the Harissa infused olive oil and all the bright flavors that come from the Aleppo Spice. With the Syrian Red Pepper Paste and bright sweetness of the mango, they combine to make this something special. This dish is typical of the meals you'd enjoy at the Syrian seaside, where the country borders the Mediterranean Sea. It is perfect with Braised Beans with Aleppo Spices (page 87) on the side, or to as part of a summer picnic by the sea (if you have access to a barbecue) accompanied by a variety of salads.

———————

Line a baking tray with parchment paper.

Dice the onion and slice the garlic thinly. Place 2 Tbsp of olive oil in a frying pan over medium heat and sauté the onions and garlic for 5–10 minutes, until just translucent. Sprinkle with the sea salt and continue to sauté for 3–4 minutes, until just golden brown. Add the balsamic and deglaze the pan, scraping up any bits that may have stuck and stirring until the vinegar is fully absorbed. Turn down the heat to low.

Meanwhile, dice the bell pepper. Add this to the onion mixture, then add the red pepper paste, tomato paste, and Aleppo spice, stirring well to combine. The mixture will now be quite thick. Remove from the heat and stir in the breadcrumbs and walnuts to form a thick, crumbly mixture.

Preheat the oven to 375°F.

Wash and pat dry the fish. Rub it all over with the remaining 2 Tbsp of the olive oil and set it on the prepared baking tray.

Evenly cover the top of the fish with the walnut crumble. Do not press it down too much, as you want it to have some texture.

SERVES
FOUR

4 Tbsp Harissa infused olive oil

1 white onion

2 garlic cloves

1 tsp sea salt

2 Tbsp Mango white balsamic vinegar

1 red bell pepper

2 Tbsp Syrian Red Pepper Paste (page 15)

2 Tbsp tomato paste

2 Tbsp Aleppo Spice (page 13)

¼ cup dried bread crumbs

¼ cup finely chopped walnuts + extra for garnish

1 (2 lb) or 4 (½ lb each) white fish fillets (cod, sea bass, or red snapper work well here)

Bake for 15–20 minutes. (Check after 15 minutes if you're using individual fillets and around 20 minutes if the fillet is whole.) You'll know the fish is done when it's bright white and beginning to flake when touched with a fork.

Remove from the oven, garnish with parsley and some extra walnuts if desired. Serve immediately.

This is delicious with classic Aleppian rice pilaf (page 29), potato salad (page 73), roasted cauliflower salad (page 75), or carrot salad (page 79).

The cooked fish will keep in an airtight container in the fridge for up to 3 days. The crumble will store well in an airtight container for up to 1 week in the fridge.

SHAWARMA

The word *shawarma* evolved from a Turkish word meaning "to turn." Traditionally, it is made with chicken, beef, lamb, goat, or turkey—or a combination. The meat is marinated and then placed on a spit to cook all day long. As the meat on the outside crisps, it's shaved off with a sharp knife to be eaten while the next layer of meat cooks. Traditionally, the spits were horizontal and rotated over a charcoal or wood fire. Nowadays, in restaurants, the spits are vertical and rotate in front of a large burner. Both of these methods are challenging to replicate at home. Here I've roasted the meat in the oven or slow cooker to absorb all the flavor of the marinade, then broiled it after its pulled to crisp it up and create a version that is tasty and easy to accomplish at the same time. It takes a bit of work but is entirely worth it. For Syrian shawarma, the meat is marinated for at least 12 hours before cooking; in many other cultures, the spices are added right before cooking. In this recipe, the Harissa infused olive oil adds a lovely warmth to the meat, and the Pomegranate dark balsamic vinegar adds depth. My favorite way to serve this is with an extra drizzle of pomegranate balsamic over the meat, along with lots of Tahini Garlic Yogurt Sauce (page 21) either over top or on the side.

SERVES
FOUR

Shawarma

½ cup Pomegranate dark balsamic vinegar, divided

¼ cup Harissa infused olive oil

2 Tbsp lemon juice

4 garlic cloves, crushed

2 Tbsp Aleppo Spice (page 13)

8 chicken thighs, bone in and skin on

1 bay leaf

1 cinnamon stick

4 cardamom pods

½ lemon

1 red onion

1 tomato

In a large bowl, whisk together ¼ cup of the balsamic, the olive oil, lemon juice, garlic, and Aleppo spice. Add the chicken and turn to coat it well in the marinade. Carefully lift the skin of the chicken and rub some of the marinade under the skin. Cover tightly, or transfer to a resealable plastic bag and let it marinate in the fridge for at least 12 hours, or up to 24 hours. (Or toss it in the freezer in its marinade for up to 3 months, and then when you're

wanting some shawarma you can take it out of the freezer and let it marinate as it thaws.)

Preheat the oven to 375°F.

Place the chicken and the marinade in a roasting pan just large enough to hold the chicken without crowding. Add the bay leaf, cinnamon stick, and cardamom. Slice the lemon into wedges and add that to the pan as well, nestling the wedges among the chicken. Roughly chop the onion and tomato and scatter them over the chicken.

Cover the pan and bake for 45 minutes, until the chicken is tender and cooked through. (This can also be done in a slow cooker on low for 6 hours.)

Remove the chicken from the oven, uncover, and let rest 5 minutes. With a fork, carefully move the onion and tomato off the chicken, remove the skin from the thighs, carefully pull the meat off the bones, and place the meat on a parchment paper–lined baking tray. Spread the meat in a thin, even layer, pour 4–5 spoonfuls of juice from the pan over the chicken to moisten it, and drizzle evenly with the remaining ¼ cup of balsamic.

Place the baking tray in the top third of the oven and then turn on the broiler. As the boiler heats up it will keep the meat warm. Watch the meat carefully while it's broiling. You want it to caramelize and turn golden, without burning, about 5 minutes.

Remove from the oven and serve immediately. Use any drippings from the roasting pan as the base for your favorite chicken stock and don't forget to brush some over the flatbread before piling it high with delicious chicken.

Cooked shawarma will keep in the fridge for 3–4 days in an airtight container, or uncooked in the marinade in the freezer for up to 3 months.

There are many ways to serve shawarma—wrapped in a fresh piece of flatbread and topped with Tahini Garlic Yogurt Sauce (page 21), lettuce or cabbage, fresh tomatoes, and Pickled Turnip (page 23), or over or beside Tabbouleh Salad (page 69) or Baba Ganoush (page 41) are just two options you might want to try.

SPICED CHICKEN SKEWERS
SHISH TAOUK

With their subtle spiciness from the Harissa infused olive oil and the sweetness from the Mango white balsamic vinegar, these chicken skewers are sure to please.

SERVES
FOUR

Pat the chicken pieces dry, cut them into cubes, and place them in a resealable plastic bag.

In a small bowl, whisk together the yogurt, tomato paste, and olive oil until thick and well combined. Grate or crush the garlic cloves over top, then add the allspice, cumin, and coriander, sumac and nutmeg, and whisk to fully combine. Whisk in the balsamic and lemon juice. Pour this marinade into the bag with the chicken, close tightly, and mix it well so the chicken is fully coated. Place in the fridge for at least 1 hour, or up to 12 hours. (Or toss it in the freezer in its marinade for up to 3 months.)

Carefully thread the chicken onto eight skewers, ensuring that the pieces have enough space between them to allow the marinade to stick to the chicken, yet are close enough to touch.

TO COOK IN THE OVEN
Preheat the oven to 375°F.

Suspend the skewers over a roasting pan or baking dish, so the chicken isn't touching the bottom. Roast for 15 minutes, until the chicken is cooked through, rotating halfway through the cooking time, then broil 2–3 minutes while rotating the skewers (with an oven mitt on!) to ensure they are crisp and evenly browned.

TO COOK ON THE GRILL
Warm your grill to hot. Place the skewers on the grill and cook for 10–15 minutes, rotating the skewers halfway through the cooking time. You can store leftovers in an airtight container in the fridge for up to 3 days.

4 large skinless, boneless chicken breasts

½ cup full-fat, Greek-style thick yogurt

1 (5½ oz) can tomato paste

¼ cup Harissa infused olive oil

8 garlic cloves

1 tsp ground allspice

1 tsp ground cumin

½ tsp ground coriander

½ tsp sumac

¼ tsp ground nutmeg

2 Tbsp Mango white balsamic vinegar

2 Tbsp lemon juice

1 cup Tahini Garlic Yogurt Sauce (page 21)

Serve hot with Bulgur Salad (page 71), Pickled Turnip (page 23), and flatbread (page 25).

ROASTED CHICKEN and YOGURT SAUCE
SHAKRIYYEH

In Syria, it's quite common to find meat served in a yogurt-style soup or sauce. This dish is one such example, and it's often served on the first of the year, as some traditions believe that serving white food on the first day of the year will bring forth purity and luck.

The warmed yogurt gives a thick, rich texture to the meat and holds the flavor of the aromatics so well. Searing the chicken in the Lime fused olive oil creates a beautiful subtlety in the dish, enhancing the fragrances of the spices and adding a refreshing citrus note. Serve with rice, Roasted Cauliflower Salad (page 75), and Roasted Rice Pudding (page 123) for dessert for an all-white affair.

Preheat the oven to 375°F.

Pat the chicken legs dry, then rub them all over with the sea salt and 1 Tbsp of oil for each leg.

Chop the onion roughly and crush the garlic cloves with the back of a knife, leaving them whole. Place them in a roasting pan, just large enough to hold everything without crowding, sprinkle with the Aleppo pepper, and then scatter the bay leaves, cloves, cardamom, and cinnamon sticks over top. Pour in the chicken stock. It should cover the bottom of the pan. Place the chicken legs on the onion spice mixture so they are snug in the pan.

Cover the pan loosely and roast for 20 minutes. Uncover the pan and roast the chicken for an additional 10 minutes, until golden brown. Remove from the oven and let rest in the drippings, covered again, to stay warm.

While the chicken is cooking, whisk together the yogurt, cornstarch, and salt in a medium bowl until smooth, creamy, and lump-free.

SERVES
FOUR

---

4 chicken legs,
bone in and skin on

1 tsp sea salt

½ cup Lime fused olive oil,
divided

2 white onions

4 garlic cloves

1 tsp Aleppo pepper
(or ½ tsp chili flakes)

3 bay leaves

5 whole cloves

4 cardamom pods

2 cinnamon sticks

½–1 cup chicken stock

3 cups full-fat, Greek-style
thick yogurt

2 Tbsp cornstarch

Pinch of sea salt

Fresh mint leaves and Aleppo
pepper or chili flakes for garnish

Tip up the roasting pan and begin to whisk the 1 cup of the pan drippings into the yogurt mixture a few tablespoons at a time.

In a heavy-bottomed frying pan over medium heat, pour in the yogurt mixture. Stirring constantly in the same direction, bring the yogurt mixture to a boil. Allow to boil for 1 minute then remove from the heat. Add the chicken pieces and return to the stovetop. Simmer on low heat for 2–3 minutes to ensure they are still warm.

Serve the chicken in a shallow bowl or rimmed plate with yogurt sauce poured around it, drizzle liberally with remaining olive oil, and garnish with fresh mint and pepper flakes.

If you're looking for an even heartier option, add a few stuffed meatballs (page 45) to the yogurt sauce as soon as it begins to boil.

You can store this in an airtight container in the fridge for up to 3 days.

Use yogurt that is fresh and has a high fat content, and slowly bring it up to temperature to ensure that it doesn't separate.

EGGPLANT with MINCED LAMB and POMEGRANATE

This recipe is a total favorite of mine. Silky smooth eggplant paired with spicy rich minced meat and topped with a bright burst of pomegranate and fresh mint, this dish is a prime example of simple ingredients working together to create a fantastic whole. The spicy Harissa infused olive oil flavors the eggplants as they roast, the Pomegranate dark balsamic vinegar adds a sweet richness to the lamb, and the creamy garlic yogurt sauce guarantees a refreshing, smooth end to each mouthful. Bliss in a dish!

Preheat the oven to 400°F.

Slice each eggplant lengthwise, leaving the tops and stems intact to use as little handles. Trim any longer green pieces from the bottom of the stems, if needed. Sprinkle 2 tsp of the salt over the eggplants and let stand for 10 minutes while the eggplant sweats. Wipe dry, use 2 Tbsp of the olive oil to brush all the cut sides, then sprinkle with remaining salt, the cumin, and pepper.

Drizzle 1 Tbsp of the remaining olive oil on a roasting pan or baking tray, place the eggplants, cut side up, on the pan, and roast for 15–20 minutes, until soft and starting to golden. Remove from the oven and brush the cut sides of the eggplant with the remaining 1 Tbsp olive oil, flip the eggplant over so they are cut side down, and bake for another 15 minutes, or until golden and almost bronzed on the bottom. (I don't line my pan for this, but it's also a well-loved, well-seasoned pan. If you have any concerns about sticking, line your pan with foil or parchment.) Remove from the oven and carefully flip over and let rest.

SERVES
FOUR

4 small eggplants

3 tsp sea salt, divided

4 Tbsp Harissa infused olive oil

1 tsp ground cumin

½ tsp cracked black pepper

1 small red onion

2 garlic cloves

1 lb ground lamb

2 tsp Aleppo Spice (page 13)

½ tsp cracked black pepper

¼ cup Pomegranate dark balsamic vinegar

2 Tbsp tomato paste

1 recipe Tahini Garlic Yogurt Sauce (page 21)

2 Tbsp fresh chopped mint leaves

¼ cup pomegranate arils

While the eggplant is cooking prepare the filling.

Dice the onion and mince the garlic. Place them in a frying pan over medium-high heat with the lamb and sauté for 3–4 minutes, breaking up the lamb as it cooks, until the onions are starting to soften and the lamb is beginning to brown and sizzle. Sprinkle in the Aleppo spice, salt, and pepper. Sauté for 2–3 more minutes, then pour in the balsamic and cook until all the liquid is absorbed and reduced, 5–7 minutes. The meat should be saucy but not runny. Mix in the tomato paste and sauté for 1–2 minutes to ensure it's fully incorporated, then remove from the heat.

Using a sharp knife, gently make two parallel slices along the length of the eggplant, being careful not to cut all the way through, and at least ½ inch away from the edges of the skin on each side. Using a fork or spoon, gently pull the flesh apart along these slices, making little troughs in the eggplant. Transfer the eggplants to serving dishes, top each one with the minced lamb, filling the troughs and piling a little over top, but still allowing the skin and beautiful golden eggplant to show.

Top the meat generously with garlic yogurt sauce, sprinkle with fresh mint and pomegranate seeds, and serve with classic Aleppian rice pilaf (page 29), braised beans with Aleppo spices (page 87), and extra yogurt sauce on the side.

LAMB SHANKS with FREEKEH PILAF
MOZAT BEL FREEKEH

One of the most common meats enjoyed in Syria, lamb is integrated into everything from street food to the most sacred and special holiday meals. Lamb shanks are a particularly tough part of the animal, although when they're cooked slowly, the connective tissue tenderizes and the meat literally falls off the bone. This recipe is great for the slow cooker, although it's equally delicious braised in the oven. Spiced and so flavorful, the lamb pairs perfectly with the freekeh pilaf. Freekeh is a green durum wheat whose chaff is burned off, creating an incredibly nutty and smoky-flavored grain.

SERVES
FOUR

4 (around 1 lb each) lamb shanks

5 Tbsp Aleppo Spice (page 13)

3 tsp sea salt

½ cup Harissa infused olive oil

2 red onions

6 garlic cloves

½ cup fresh chopped
flat-leaf parsley

¼ cup fresh chopped mint leaves

1 (19 oz) can diced tomatoes

¼ cup lemon juice
(about 2 large lemons)

1 bay leaf

1 cinnamon stick

10 black peppercorns

5 cardamom pods

2 Tbsp Lime fused olive oil

2 cups freekeh

¼ cup Pomegranate dark
balsamic vinegar

4 cups beef or vegetable stock

Garnish

fresh mint

curly-leaf parsley

Pat dry the lamb shanks. Mix 4 Tbsp of the Aleppo spice with 2 tsp of the sea salt. Rub each lamb shank with 1 heaping Tbsp of the Aleppo spice-salt blend.

Heat 2 Tbsp of the Harissa infused olive oil over medium-high heat in a heavy-bottomed frying pan or Dutch oven. Sear each of the lamb shanks, one at a time to avoid overcrowding the pan and adding 2 Tbsp of oil each time, until browned fully.

Remove the shanks from the pan and set aside, leaving the residue oil and drippings in the pan. Do not wipe out the pan.

Chop 1 of the onions and crush 4 of the garlic cloves with the back of a knife, keeping the cloves in one piece. Add these to the pan with the olive oil and lamb drippings. Sauté over medium-high heat for 3–5 minutes, just until golden and soft. Add the parsley and mint, sauté for 2–3 minutes, until they just start to lose their color. Pour the juice from the can of tomatoes into the pan, then gently crush the tomatoes in your hand before adding them to the pan with the lemon juice. Stir to combine and bring to a boil, then remove from the heat.

Preheat the oven to 375°F.

If you're using a Dutch oven to make the braise, place the lamb shanks in the sauce.

If not, arrange the lamb shanks in a roasting pan just large enough to hold them without crowding and pour the sauce over top.

Whichever method you're using, now add the bay leaf, cinnamon stick, peppercorns, and cardamom pods, and fill the pan with enough water to just cover the meat. Cover the pan and roast the lamb for 2 hours, or until the meat is tender and falling off the bone.

When the lamb has been in the oven for about an hour, dice the remaining onion and finely chop the remaining cloves of garlic. In a heavy-bottomed saucepan, heat the Lime fused olive oil over medium heat and sauté the onion and garlic 2–3 minutes, until just translucent. Add the remaining 1 Tbsp of Aleppo spice and 1 tsp of salt, then sauté for 2–3 minutes, until golden. Add the freekeh, and sauté 2–3 minutes until any remaining liquid has been absorbed and the grains are glossy. Pour in the balsamic to deglaze the pan and allow the freekeh to absorb the vinegar and all the amazing flavors. When all the balsamic has been absorbed, 2–3 minutes, pour in the stock, cook for 1 minute, then turn down the heat to low, and simmer, partially covered, until the freekeh is tender, 30–45 minutes.

When ready to serve, remove the lamb shanks from the oven and let sit for 5 minutes in their cooking liquid to cool slightly. Fluff the pilaf and spread it on a serving platter. Arrange the shanks over top the pilaf and spoon over some of the sauce to keep the meat moist. Garnish with fresh mint and parsley and serve with thick, Greek-style, full-fat yogurt on the side.

You can store the lamb and the pilaf separately in airtight containers in the fridge for up to 3 days.

SWEETS

ATAYEF

Stuffed with smooth strained yogurt cheese and drenched in a floral syrup, these pancakes are a classic Syrian dessert. The trick is to work quickly after the pancakes have baked so that the edges easily stick together—you can leave one end open or close both ends. Whisking the Lime fused olive oil into the batter and the Mango white balsamic vinegar into the strained yogurt cheese makes for a delicious fruity combination, making this amazing dish even more delectable.

Preheat the oven to 200°F. Place an ovenproof plate on the center rack.

In a large bowl, whisk together the flour, sugar, baking powder, baking soda, and salt. Make a well in the center of this mixture and add the milk, egg, and olive oil. Whisk the oil, egg and milk together briefly (it's ok if some of the dry ingredients get whisked in), then mix in the dry ingredients, forming a smooth light batter (a few lumps are okay).

Heat a non-stick frying pan over medium heat. It must be evenly warmed.

Pour in ¼ cup of batter, forming a 6-inch circle in the pan. Fry until bubbles start to form on the top, the edges are crisp, and the underside is golden, 2–3 minutes. With a spatula or lifter, transfer the pancake and place it, batter side up, on the plate in the oven. Repeat with the remaining batter.

Whisk together the strained yogurt cheese and 2 Tbsp of the balsamic. Set aside.

Place the sugar and water in a small saucepan over high heat. Bring to a rolling boil and boil for 2 minutes, then remove from the heat, and whisk in the remaining 2 Tbsp balsamic, and the rose and orange blossom

SERVES
FOUR

Makes 12–16 pancakes

1 cup all-purpose flour

2 Tbsp granulated sugar

1½ tsp baking powder

½ tsp baking soda

½ tsp sea salt

1 cup milk (any %)

1 egg

2 Tbsp Lime fused olive oil

1 cup Strained Yogurt Cheese (page 17) (or mascarpone)

4 Tbsp Mango white balsamic vinegar

1 cup granulated sugar

½ cup water

1 tsp rosewater

½ tsp orange blossom water

Edible rose petals for garnish (optional)

waters. Remove from the heat and allow to cool just enough to handle.

To assemble the pancakes, remove from the oven and place 1 Tbsp of cream in the center of the pancake. Gently press together the edges of the pancake to create a half-moon shape around the strained yogurt cheese, encasing it completely. (You might need to sprinkle a little water on the edges of the pancake to make them stick.) Place on a parchment paper–covered baking sheet or a serving plate. Repeat with the remaining pancakes.

To serve the filled pancakes warm, just before serving place them in a frying pan over medium heat in some extra virgin or Lime fused olive oil for 1–2 minutes per side. Drench in syrup and serve with a sprinkling of rose petals for garnish, if desired.

These pancakes don't keep well in the fridge, although they do freeze extremely well. You can store them in an airtight container in the freezer for up to 3 months and fry from frozen then drench in the syrup before serving. To fry from frozen, increase the cooking time to 3–4 minutes. I also like to warm the syrup a bit before serving them this way.

MILK and MANGO PUDDING

Layered desserts with vibrant colors are always attractive, and guests will never know how easy they were to toss together!

SERVES
FOUR

1 cup whole milk

½ cup granulated sugar

4 Tbsp cornstarch

1 cup whipping (35%) cream

2 Tbsp Lime fused olive oil

2 mangos or 2 cups frozen mango pieces (left out to thaw)

2 Tbsp Mango white balsamic vinegar

2 Tbsp lime juice and grated zest for garnish

Bring the milk to a simmer in a heavy-bottomed saucepan over medium heat. Mix together the sugar and half the cornstarch to make a lump-free powder. Place the cream in a measuring jug, add olive oil, and whisk in the sugar-cornstarch mix to combine.

Whisking constantly, pour the cream mixture into the simmering milk, increase the temperature to high, and bring to a boil, stirring constantly. Let it boil for 1 minute and then remove from the heat. Pour immediately, dividing it evenly between four dessert glasses or cups, and place in the fridge to cool completely, uncovered, for at least 2 hours.

Peel and chop the flesh of the mango if you're using fresh or drain off any water from the frozen mango pieces, and place the mango in a blender or small food processor. Purée until smooth.

Whisk together the remaining 2 Tbsp of cornstarch, the balsamic, and lime juice to form a creamy paste. Transfer the mango purée to a medium saucepan over medium-high heat and whisk in the cornstarch mixture. Bring to a boil, whisking constantly. Allow to boil for 1 minute and then remove from the heat and allow to cool for 10 minutes.

Remove the dessert cups from the fridge. Divide the mango mixture evenly over top of the milk pudding, then let cool completely in the fridge, uncovered, for 2–3 hours.

Garnish with some finely grated lime zest. You can store these, covered, in the fridge for up to 1 week.

ROASTED RICE PUDDING

Simple and classic, this rose-scented rice pudding offers sweet comfort when served warm and a refreshing bite when served chilled. This is a dessert that I love to put in the oven, moments before sitting down to enjoy dinner. It cooks while we eat and talk and fills the kitchen with beautiful fragrances. As soon as we're done eating our main meal, the table is cleared, the pudding comes out of the oven, and tea is served! Whisking the Lime fused olive oil into the rice before it is baked intensifies the flavor of the rice and is the perfect complement to the rosewater. I love to garnish this with rose petals and lime zest to add a touch of color.

Preheat the oven to 325°F.

Rinse the rice well, shaking off any excess water, then place it in a small saucepan over medium heat. Pour in 3 Tbsp of the olive oil and stir to combine. Cook until the rice is glossy and translucent, 2–3 minutes, and then remove from the heat. Drizzle the remaining 1 Tbsp olive oil in a glass or ceramic baking dish and rub to coat evenly. Add the rice, stir in the sugar so it's evenly distributed, and then pour in the milk, cream, and rosewater.

Cover the pan partially with a lid or cover loosely with foil, leaving an opening on the side for some of the steam to escape.

Bake for 1 hour, then uncover and bake for an additional 15 minutes. Spoon warm pudding into bowls and garnish with lime zest and rose petals, and a drizzle of extra cream if desired. Alternatively, let it chill completely in the fridge and serve cold.

You can store this in an airtight container in the fridge for up to 3 days. This dish does not freeze well.

SERVES
FOUR

---

1 cup short-grain rice

4 Tbsp Lime fused olive oil, divided

½ cup granulated sugar

2 cups whole milk

1 cup whipping (35%) cream

3 Tbsp rosewater

Lime zest, rose petals, and cream for garnish

MANGO CARDAMOM ORANGE BLOSSOM JAM

Sweet, tart, and floral, this jam is delicious on toast with a dollop of cream cheese, lovely paired with ice cream or sorbet, and super tasty when used as a glaze for cakes and cookies. The Mango white balsamic vinegar adds a brightness to the already sweet mango pulp and lends balance to the intensity of the floral flavors.

———————————

Place the mango pulp, sugar, balsamic, cardamom, and sea salt in a large, heavy-bottomed saucepan and bring to a rolling boil over high heat. Let boil for 1 minute and then stir in the liquid pectin.

Remove from the heat and stir constantly for 1 minute. Add in the olive oil and continue to stir for about another minute, until fully incorporated. Stir in the orange blossom water and rosewater, then stir again to combine fully. Pour the jam into clean mason jars, leaving ¼ inch of headspace at the top of each jar. Put the lid and ring on tightly and let rest in a cool place until sealed. (You'll hear the lid pop when it seals, and you'll be able to feel an indent in the top of the lid after it's sealed.)

Refrigerate after opening. This will last up to one year, unopened, in a cool dark cupboard or up to 6 months, once opened, in the fridge.

Makes 4 cups

3½ cups mango pulp

3 cup granulated sugar

¼ cup Mango white balsamic vinegar

2 tsp ground cardamom

1 tsp sea salt

1 (6 oz) packet liquid pectin

1 Tbsp Lime fused olive oil

2 tsp orange blossom water

1 tsp rosewater

To make 3½ cups of mango pulp, dice four to five mangos, or chop 4 cups of loosely packed thawed mango cubes. Place them in a blender or food processor and pulse a few times to break up the flesh, leaving a few chunky bits but not too much.

NUT-FILLED COOKIES with CARDAMOM COFFEE
MAMOOLS

Simplicity at its best, these lovely milk cookies filled with walnuts are found everywhere in bake shops across Syria. Typically, wooden molds are used to create lovely patterns on the outside of the dough, but the cookies taste just as good without the patterns. The Lime fused olive oil in both the nut filling and the pastry adds a lovely flavor throughout the cookie. The mango, which isn't a traditional addition to these, adds an extra brightness to the filling, making this version a favorite to pair with traditional cardamom coffee for an after-dinner sweet or afternoon pick-me-up.

———————————

To make the cookies, place the walnuts, 2 Tbsp of the olive oil, ¾ cup of the sugar, the balsamic, and orange blossom water in a bowl and mix well. Set aside to allow the walnuts to soak while you make the dough.

In a large mixing bowl, whisk together both flours, the baking powder, salt, cardamom, cinnamon, cloves, and nutmeg. Make a well in the center and pour in the remaining 6 Tbsp of olive oil and the milk, and mix until you have a soft dough. (I like to use my hands for this, but a wooden spoon also works well.)

Preheat the oven to 375°F. Line a baking sheet with parchment paper.

Divide the dough into 24 evenly sized pieces and form each one into a ball. Using your fingers, press a hole in the center of each ball and spoon 1 heaping Tbsp of walnut filling into it. Pull the edges together to seal in the filling, then press each cookie gently seam side down onto the prepared baking sheet so the cookies have a flat bottom and a little dome on top.

Bake for 15 minutes, until lightly golden and crisp. Remove from the oven and allow to cool completely on a wire baking rack before serving. The nuts will hold their

Makes 2 dozen cookies

Cookies
2 cups chopped walnuts
½ cup Lime fused olive oil, divided
1½ cups granulated sugar, divided
¼ cup Mango white balsamic vinegar
2 Tbsp orange blossom water
2 cups all-purpose flour
1 cup fine ground semolina flour
1 tsp baking powder
½ tsp sea salt
½ tsp ground cardamom
¼ tsp ground cinnamon
Pinch ground cloves
Pinch ground nutmeg
1 cup whole milk
Icing sugar for dusting

Cardamom coffee
¼ cup finely ground espresso powder
1 Tbsp ground cardamom
Pinch of sea salt

heat, so be careful if you decide to sneak one straight from the oven. Once cooled, dust with icing sugar before serving, if desired.

TO MAKE THE COFFEE

Mix together the espresso, cardamom, and salt in a small bowl to form a very fine, heavily scented mixture. Place it in a very fine tea strainer or a coffee filter-lined strainer set over a small glass liquid measuring cup. (You need to be able to place your strainer into the cup.) Pour 1 cup of just-boiled water over the coffee grounds. Very carefully, whisk the grounds with the water for 30 seconds, then pull the strainer out of the water. Hold it above the water in the cup and allow the remaining water to drain from the strainer.

When the water is done dripping from the grounds, place the strainer back in the water and whisk again for 30 seconds. Repeat this whisking and draining process until you've done it a total of 3–5 times, until the coffee is well steeped and strong. Discard the coffee granules. Pour the coffee into espresso cups and serve immediately with sugar on the side (if desired).

You can store the cookies in an airtight container on the counter for 2–3 days, or in the fridge for up to 1 week. You can also freeze the baked cookies in an airtight container for up to 3 months. When you're ready to eat them, let them thaw completely and pop in the oven for 3 minutes at 350°F to crisp up again and warm through.

DATE SANDWICH COOKIES

Let's be honest, sandwich cookies, as lovely as they are to look at and eat, are a bit of a pain to make. Rolling and cutting out the dough, baking the pieces, then assembling everything requires a real time commitment. Rest assured that these date cookies are well worth the effort, and they also store really well, so one Sunday afternoon of baking will give you at least a week's worth of cookies to enjoy with tea or coffee for an afternoon snack, or after-dinner treats. The Pomegranate dark balsamic vinegar adds a lovely rich, yet not overly sweet, flavor and tempers the sugary dates. The Lime fused olive oil in the cookie completes the gastronomic picture.

———————

To make the dough, sift together the flour, baking powder, and salt in a medium-sized bowl. In a separate large bowl, or in the bowl of a stand mixer fitted with the paddle attachment, cream the butter and olive oil with the sugar until light and fluffy. With the mixer running, add 1 egg at a time, beating well between additions. With the machine running on its lowest setting, begin to beat in the flour, ½ cup at a time, allowing it to be fully incorporated before adding the next ½ cup. The dough will be stiff and a little sticky. Cover with plastic wrap and place in the fridge for at least 1 hour, or up to overnight.

To make the date filling, finely chop the pitted dates and place them in a small pan with the ⅓ cup water. Pour in the balsamic, orange zest, orange blossom water, and spices, then simmer over low heat, all the while pressing together the dates to allow them to soften and form a thick paste, 7–10 minutes. Remove from the heat and allow to cool completely in the pan.

Remove the dough from the fridge and cut it in half. Place one half on a floured counter and wrap the other

Makes 3 dozen cookies

Dough

5 cups all-purpose flour

2 tsp baking powder

½ tsp sea salt

½ cup granulated sugar

¾ cup unsalted butter, soft

½ cup Lime fused olive oil

5 eggs

Date Filling

¾ cup pitted dates

⅓ cup water

2 Tbsp Pomegranate dark balsamic vinegar

1 tsp grated orange zest

½ tsp orange blossom water

½ tsp ground cardamom

¼ tsp ground cinnamon

and put it back in the fridge. Dust the top of the dough and your rolling pin with flour. Roll out the dough to ¼ inch thick.

Preheat the oven to 400°F. Line a baking sheet with parchment paper.

Cut out circles 1–1½ inch in diameter (use a fluted cutter, if you prefer) and place each one on the prepared baking sheet, 1 inch apart. It's best to only have one baking sheet at a time in the oven for these, so you may have to bake them in batches.

Bake for 10–12 minutes, until crisp and starting to golden. Remove from the oven and allow to cool completely on a wire rack. Reroll, cut, and bake any remaining dough from the first batch. Count the number of cookie bases you have.

Remove the second half of dough from the fridge and repeat the process above, but this time you also want to use a small round cutter to cut a hole in the center of each cookie. Do your best to match the numbers of tops and bottoms so each cookie has a bottom and a lid too.

When both the cookies and the date mixture are cool, place 1 tsp of date filling on the base of each cookie, top with a lid, and press down gently, allowing the filling to spread right to the edges of each cookie.

You can store these in an airtight container for up to 1 week. These cookies also freeze very well before baking and filling. Once you've cut them out, freeze the raw dough and bake from frozen. The baking time may need to be increased by 1–2 minutes.

Yes, you did see butter listed in this recipe! Mixing it with the olive oil keeps the cookies from spreading too much during baking. What can I say? Even I have to reach for the butter on occasion.

BAKLAWA CIGARS

This simple version of baklava, filled with chopped nuts and a lovely floral syrup, isn't as sweet or messy to eat as the classic version. Rolling the filling into smaller cookies lets you make small bites that are easier to eat. The Lime fused olive oil is the perfect addition to soak into the phyllo pastry and complement the nuttiness of the cookies.

Preheat the oven to 350°F.

Finely chop the 1 cup of nuts and place them in a medium-sized bowl. Add 2 Tbsp of the olive oil and then ¼ cup of the sugar and stir to coat the nuts well. Set aside.

In a small saucepan over medium heat, whisk the remaining sugar with ½ cup of water. Bring to a boil over medium-high heat, stirring constantly for 1 minute, then remove from the heat. Whisk in the rosewater and balsamic, and then set aside to cool slightly.

Line a baking sheet with parchment paper and place it beside you. Place the remaining 6 Tbsp of olive oil in a small bowl with a pastry brush. Place the cooled rosewater syrup in a separate small bowl with its own pastry brush.

Unroll the stack of phyllo pastry, but don't separate the sheets. Brush a thin, even layer of olive oil over the entire top sheet of phyllo. Then brush the entire sheet again lightly and evenly with the warm rosewater syrup.

Sprinkle about 2 Tbsp of the nut mixture in a narrow line about 1 inch away from the edge of the phyllo. Grasp two sheets of the phyllo pastry (you need a double layer) and gently roll them up, over the nuts, to form a tube. Carefully transfer to the prepared baking sheet and cut in half, creating two cigar-shaped cookies. Scrunch or gently push the ends together on each cookie, creating a slight wrinkle effect in the dough. Repeat with the remaining phyllo.

Makes 2 dozen cookies

1 cup plus 2 Tbsp shelled pistachios, divided

½ cup Lime fused olive oil, divided

1¼ cups granulated sugar, divided

½ cup water

2 tsp rosewater

1 tsp Mango white balsamic vinegar

24 sheets of phyllo pastry, thawed

In Syria, pistachios are traditionally used, but feel free to use walnuts, pecans, almonds, or a combination if you prefer.

Bake for 10–12 minutes, until golden brown and crisp. Remove from the oven, and immediately brush the outside of each cigar cookie with more rose syrup. (You can gently rewarm the syrup before doing this.) Garnish with pistachio crumbs if desired.

You can store these in an airtight container at room temperature for up to 1 week. Do not store in the fridge, as the pastry will go soggy. You can also freeze these before baking them. Flash-freeze them on the baking sheet and then transfer them to airtight containers to keep in the freezer for up to 3 months. Bake directly from frozen and increase baking time by 5 minutes.

SPICED SEMOLINA CAKE

Sometimes this cake is called Harissa (not to be confused with the lovely spicy red pepper paste or olive oil used in these pages). It's soaked with an amazing floral syrup and, the flavor is given an extra hint of brightness thanks to the Lime fused olive oil, which also adds a soft touch. This cake is also the ideal vehicle to show how Aleppo Spice (page 13) can be used to delicious effect in sweet dishes. The semolina gives this cake a lovely crumb—do use the finest ground semolina flour you can find for best results. If you can only find a coarse ground semolina flour, you can soak it in the milk for a few hours before adding it to the batter to soften it slightly.

Preheat the oven to 375°F. Lightly grease a 9-inch baking pan with a little extra virgin olive oil and dust it with flour. Set aside.

To make the cake, in a large mixing bowl, whisk together the eggs, sugar, and olive oil until pale yellow and fluffy. Slowly whisk in the yogurt until the mixture is completely lump-free and then, with the machine running, pour in the milk to form a very loose batter.

Place the all-purpose flour, baking powder, baking soda, Aleppo spice, and cardamom in a bowl, mix to combine, and then sift half of the mixture over the batter. Whisk to fully incorporate, and then sift in the remaining flour, whisking again to incorporate fully. Add the semolina ½ cup at a time, whisking between each addition to incorporate fully.

Pour the batter into the prepared cake pan and tap the pan gently on the counter to even out the batter and remove any air bubbles. Bake for 45–50 minutes, until golden and a toothpick inserted in the center comes out clean.

Makes 2 (8-inch) round cakes or one (9- × 13-inch) cake

Cake
3 eggs

¾ cup granulated sugar

½ cup Lime fused olive oil

1 cup full-fat, Greek-style thick yogurt

1 cup milk

1 cup all-purpose flour

2 tsp baking powder

½ tsp baking soda

1½ tsp Aleppo Spice (page 13)

½ tsp ground cardamom

2 cups fine ground semolina flour or farina

Syrup
1 cup granulated sugar

½ cup water

1 tsp rosewater

½ tsp orange blossom water

While the cake is baking, make the syrup. Whisk together the sugar and water in a small saucepan and bring to a rolling boil over high heat. Let boil for 1 minute, then remove from the heat. Whisk in the rose and orange blossom waters.

As soon as the cake comes out of the oven, run a knife around the edges of the pan to loosen the cake, but leave it in the pan. Using a toothpick or small skewer, prick the cake all over its surface. Pour the syrup over the cake (it's okay if it has cooled by now), using a pastry brush or spoon to ensure it's evenly distributed over the cake. Allow the cake to sit for at least an hour to cool and to allow the syrup to fully soak in before serving.

You can store this in an airtight container at room temperature for up to 1 week or freeze it for up to 3 months.

HALVAH

This sesame candy is nutty, slightly crumbly, and perfect served with some flatbread for afternoon tea. Its nutty aroma and sweetness are brightened by the Mango white balsamic vinegar and complemented by the Lime fused olive oil, which adds a mild acidity and freshness without being overpowering. The oil also prevents the halvah from sticking to the pan. Almost any dish can be used to make this, but I love to use a loaf tin—it's the perfect size and the halvah is easy to remove from it. Often this will have pistachios, or a variety of other nuts, added, but I decided to keep this version simple with lime zest and pomegranate seeds for a pop of color. If you want to use nuts, stir in 1 cup of chopped nuts right before you spoon the mixture into the prepared baking dish.

In a small saucepan over high heat, mix together the sugar and water and stir once. Bring to a boil, stirring more frequently now, and cook the sugar, keeping it at a boil, until it evenly coats the back of a spoon, 2–3 minutes. Remove from the heat and whisk in the balsamic.

Whisk in the tahini, ½ cup at a time, until fully incorporated, then whisk in 1 Tbsp of the olive oil and the ginger.

Grease a loaf tin with the remaining 1 Tbsp olive oil and pour in the tahini mixture, smoothing the top with the back of a spoon. Place in the fridge, uncovered, and chill until completely set, 3–4 hours.

Remove from the fridge, turn the loaf tin upside down, and gently tap the bottom with a wooden spoon. The halvah should just pop out. Garnish with pomegranate arils.

Wrap any leftovers tightly in plastic wrap and store in an airtight container for up to 3 weeks in the fridge, or in the freezer for up to 3 months.

*Makes 2½ cups
(one 8- × 4-inch loaf pan)*

1 cup granulated sugar

¼ cup water

2 Tbsp Mango white balsamic vinegar

2 cups tahini

1½ Tbsp Lime fused olive oil, divided

½ tsp ground ginger

Pomegranate arils for garnish

Halvah is a sweet sesame seed paste and is known in various parts of the Middle East as *halawa, alva, haleweh, halava, helava, helva, halwa, halua, aluva, chalva,* or *chałwa!*

SWEET CHEESE ROLL with ROSE PETAL JAM
HALAWET EL JEBEN

This unique dessert is a delicious mix of cheesecake and jelly roll. Traditionally served during Ramadan, it's sure to please everyone at the table. It's also normally made in bite-sized pieces, but I decided to make it into one large roll. To be truly authentic, you should use a Middle Eastern cheese called Akkawi, but it is very hard to find in North America. Luckily, mozzarella works really well as a substitute. The Lime fused olive oil softens the already soft dough and ensures that it rolls easily. The Mango white balsamic vinegar is a delightful addition to the subtle tastes provided by the rose and orange blossom water in the syrup. I do love to whisk a little into the strained yogurt cheese to give it a bright pop as well.

———————————

To make the syrup, place the sugar and water in a small, heavy-bottomed, high-sided saucepan over high heat and bring to a rolling boil. Let boil for 1 minute and then remove from the heat. Whisk in the balsamic, orange blossom water, and rose water. Allow to cool completely, then transfer to a jar or jug until you're ready to use it. This can be stored in an airtight container in the fridge for up to 3 months. Feel free to double the recipe to keep extra on hand. It's not only commonly found in Syrian desserts, it also works well as a simple syrup in cocktails.

To make the dough, pour the water and sugar into in a large, heavy-bottomed saucepan, bring to a boil over medium-high heat and then immediately turn down the heat to medium. Slowly sprinkle in the semolina, whisking constantly, until the dough starts to pull away from the sides of the saucepan. As it thickens, you'll need to switch to stirring with a spoon.

Still stirring, gradually sprinkle in 1 cup of the cheese, pour in 1 Tbsp of the olive oil, and then sprinkle in the remaining 1 cup cheese. As the cheese melts it will loosen

SERVES
SIX–EIGHT
———

Syrup
1 cup granulated sugar

½ cup water

1 tsp Mango white balsamic vinegar

½ tsp orange blossom water

½ tsp rosewater

Dough
1 cup water

½ cup granulated sugar

1 cup fine ground semolina flour

2 cups shredded mozzarella, divided

2 Tbsp Lime fused olive oil

1 tsp rosewater

1½ cups Strained Yogurt Cheese (page 17)

2 Tbsp Mango white balsamic vinegar

3 Tbsp rose petal jam

Mango Cardamom Orange Blossom Jam (page 125), edible rose petals, and grated lime zest for garnish the dough and create a thick, smooth, shiny, slightly goopy mass. Remove from the heat and let sit for 5 minutes to cool in the saucepan.

Place a piece of parchment or plastic wrap at least 9 × 13 inches on the countertop. Place the ball of dough on the parchment and drizzle it with the remaining 1 Tbsp olive oil, rubbing in slightly to coat. Let rest for another 10 minutes, until cool enough to handle, then use a rolling pin to roll the dough into a rectangle about ¼ inch thick. Using a pizza cutter or bench scraper, trim the edges to create a rectangle, about 9 × 13 inches. Allow the dough to cool completely, about 10 minutes.

Whisk the balsamic into the chilled strained yogurt cheese and spread in a thick, even layer over the surface of the rectangle, leaving a 1-inch border around the outside.

Using the parchment as a guide, carefully begin to roll up the dough, starting at one short end, to form a log. Don't push too hard on the roll (you don't want to squish the cream out the sides). Stop just before the second short end. Brush the 1-inch border at this end with a little bit of the syrup and then roll the final part of the dough to seal it. Very carefully, place the log seam side down on a baking sheet (no need to grease or line it). Drizzle half the syrup over the log, using a pastry brush to evenly coat, then place in the fridge for about 1 hour to cool completely.

When ready to serve, transfer the roll to a serving platter or board, and dot the top of it with rose petal jam and sprinkle lightly with lime zest. Cut into 1-inch slices and serve with a drizzle of syrup over each piece.

You can store this in an airtight container in the fridge for up to 3 days. You can add more syrup over top when you're ready to eat it.

Rose petal jam is found in Mediterranean grocery stores. If you can't track it down, you can use mango cardamom jam (page 125).

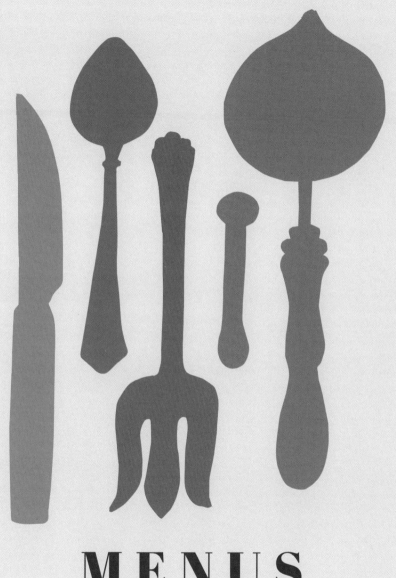

MENUS

THE
MEZZE TABLE

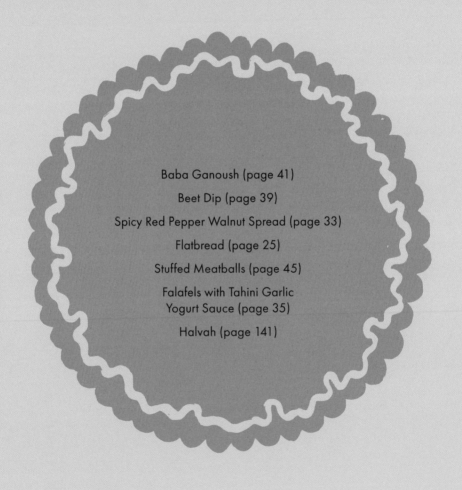

NEW YEAR'S FEAST
(ALL-WHITE-FOOD DINNER)

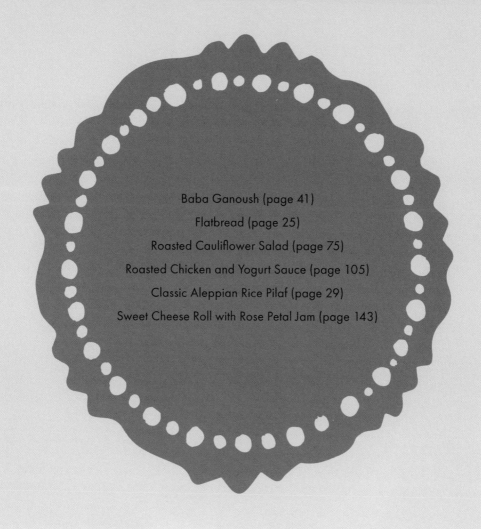

Baba Ganoush (page 41)

Flatbread (page 25)

Roasted Cauliflower Salad (page 75)

Roasted Chicken and Yogurt Sauce (page 105)

Classic Aleppian Rice Pilaf (page 29)

Sweet Cheese Roll with Rose Petal Jam (page 143)

STREET-FOOD FAVORITES

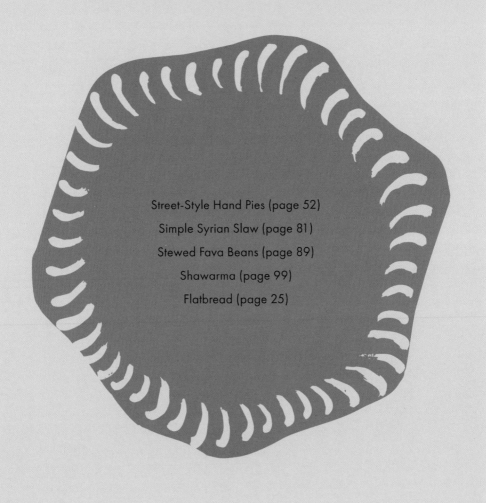

THE WINTER WARM-UP

Red Lentil and Rice Soup (page 61)

Braised Beans with Aleppo Spices
(page 87)

Eggplant with Minced Lamb
and Pomegranate (page 109)

Nut-Filled Cookies with
Cardamom Coffee (page 127)

METRIC CONVERSIONS CHART

VOLUME	
⅛ tsp	0.5 mL
¼ tsp	1 mL
½ tsp	2.5 mL
¾ tsp	4 mL
1 tsp	5 mL
1½ tsp	7.5 mL
2 tsp	10 mL
1 Tbsp	15 mL
4 tsp	20 mL
2 Tbsp	30 mL
3 Tbsp	45 mL
¼ cup/4 Tbsp	60 mL
5 Tbsp	75 mL
⅓ cup	80 mL
½ cup	125 mL
⅔ cup	160 mL
¾ cup	185 mL
1 cup	250 mL

VOLUME	
1¼ cups	310 mL
1½ cups	375 mL
1¾ cups	435 mL
2 cups/1 pint	500 mL
2¼ cups	560 mL
2½ cups	625 mL
3 cups	750 mL
3½ cups	875 mL
4 cups/1 quart	1 L
4½ cups	1.125 L
5 cups	1.25 L
5½ cups	1.375 L
6 cups	1.5 L
6½ cups	1.625 L
7 cups	1.75 L
8 cups	2 L
12 cups	3 L

VOLUME	
¼ fl oz	7.5 mL
½ fl oz	15 mL
¾ fl oz	22 mL
1 fl oz	30 mL
1½ fl oz	45 mL
2 fl oz	60 mL
3 fl oz	90 mL
4 fl oz	125 mL
5 fl oz	160 mL
6 fl oz	185 mL
8 fl oz	250 mL
24 fl oz	750 mL

WEIGHT	
1 oz	30 g
2 oz	60 g
3 oz	90 g
¼ lb/4 oz	125 g
5 oz	150 g
6 oz	175 g
½ lb/8 oz	250 g
9 oz	270 g
10 oz	300 g
¾ lb/12 oz	375 g
14 oz	400 g
1 lb	500 g
1½ lb	750 g
2 lb	1 kg
2½ lb	1.25 kg
3 lb	1.5 kg
4 lb	1.8 kg
5 lb	2.3 kg
5½ lb	2.5 kg
6 lb	2.7 kg

LENGTH	
⅛ inch	3 mm
¼ inch	6 mm
⅜ inch	9 mm
½ inch	1.25 cm
¾ inch	2 cm
1 inch	2.5 cm
1½ inches	4 cm
2 inches	5 cm
3 inches	8 cm
4 inches	10 cm
4½ inches	11 cm
5 inches	12 cm
6 inches	15 cm
7 inches	18 cm
8 inches	20 cm
8½ inches	22 cm
9 inches	23 cm
10 inches	25 cm
11 inches	28 cm
12 inches	30 cm

OVEN TEMPERATURE	
40°F	5°C
120°F	49°C
125°F	51°C
130°F	54°C
135°F	57°C
140°F	60°C
145°F	63°C
150°F	66°C
155°F	68°C
160°F	71°C
165°F	74°C
170°F	77°C
180°F	82°C
200°F	95°C
225°F	107°C
250°F	120°C
275°F	140°C
300°F	150°C
325°F	160°C
350°F	180°C
375°F	190°C
400°F	200°C
425°F	220°C
450°F	230°C
475°F	240°C
500°F	260°C

CAN SIZES	
4 oz	114 mL
14 oz	398 mL
19 oz	540 mL
28 oz	796 mL

ACKNOWLEDGMENTS

Thank you to all the friends, loved ones, and faithful customers who have inspired these recipes and have encouraged me as you've enjoyed them. As my food nerdiness evolves and my love for olive oil and vinegar deepens, I continue to be amazed at all the wonderful people in my life who lift me up and bring it all together. Thank you.

Steve, even though this is supposed to be a note of appreciation, I'll start with an apology: I'm sorry for inflicting on you dozens of test falafels and a fridge filled with bowls of coleslaw. I'm sorry for waking you up before dawn on your days off so I could catch the ferry to Salt Spring for photo shoots. I'm sorry for sending you on midnight grocery runs when I ran out of limes. Thank you for all those days when I needed you to take Cedrik so he wasn't underfoot in our little over-active kitchen; you put all the pieces together, and you make this dream a reality. Thank you for supporting my vision and walking beside me every step of the way.

Danielle, you are the best partner in crime, and these recipes would be nothing without your exceptional talent for making images come alive and jump off the page. Working with you is my favourite. I look forward to our days together and can't wait to see what comes next!

Taryn, thank you for catching our dreams, for falling in love with olive oil and vinegar, and for making the book so beautiful and vivid. If it wasn't for you and your vision, none of this would be happening. You are a rock, and you and the TouchWood team work tirelessly to bring the dream to life.

To all the Syrian families who supported this project, shared their favourite family dishes, and tasted my versions to make sure they were on the mark: thank you. This project would not be what it is without your support and the generous sharing of your love of quality ingredients, delicious food, and all the good things. We are so glad you're here sharing your culture with us.

This book also wouldn't be possible without the incredible Olive the Senses team. You are so capable and patient, and you've held down the fort right from the beginning. Thank you for letting me take time away from the daily details to make this book happen. I have deep gratitude for you for loving our customers, sharing my inspiration and passion, and running with all of it. I have learned so much from you. What we create together is the best, and none of this would be possible without you, your taste buds, fridge space, and endless energy. From the late-night cooking adventures to morning check-ins that include five versions of babaganoush, flatbread, and rice pudding, I thank you from the bottom of my heart.

INDEX

EMILY LYCOPOLUS is the owner of Olive the Senses (olivethesenses.com), a luxury olive oil and vinegar tasting room and shop in Victoria, BC, Canada, that offers the finest fresh premium olive oils and balsamic vinegars from all over the world. She is also the founder of This Table Collective (ThisTable. com), an online food community that sources artisanal food products, shares recipes and artisan stories, and supports food-focused charities.

Emily lives in Victoria with her husband, Steve, and their pug, Cedrik. She can most often be found at local markets, in her kitchen creating and testing new recipes, or else mingling in her store with her loyal customers.

DANIELLE (DL) ACKEN is a Canadian-born international food photographer who splits her time between London, UK, and her farm studio on Canada's beautiful Salt Spring Island. A self-proclaimed compulsive traveler, her photography is inspired by the multitude of palettes and moods found throughout her wanderings. See her work at dlacken.com.

Edited by Lesley Cameron
Designed and illustrated by Tree Abraham
Proofread by Claire Philipson

LIBRARY AND ARCHIVES CANADA CATALOGUING IN PUBLICATION

Lycopolus, Emily, 1985-, author
Syria : recipes for olive oil and vinegar lovers / Emily Lycopolus ; photographs by DL Acken.

Includes index.

Issued in print and electronic formats.
ISBN 978-1-77151-281-7 (hardcover). ISBN 978-1-77151-282-4 (EPUB)

1. Cooking (Olive oil). 2. Cooking (Vinegar). 3. Olive oil. 4. Vinegar. 5. Cooking,
Syrian. 6. Cookbooks. I. Title. II. Title: Recipes for olive oil and vinegar lovers.

TX819.O42L937 2018   641.6'463   C2018-902022-9
C2018-902482-8

Canadä

We acknowledge the financial support of the Government of Canada through the Canada Book
Fund and the province of British Columbia through the Book Publishing Tax Credit.

This book was produced using FSC®-certified, acid-free papers,
processed chlorine-free and printed with soya-based inks.

Printed in China

22 21 20 19 18   2 3 4 5